DON'T ASK
THE BLIND GUY
FOR
DIRECTIONS

To everyone looking for a little bit of hope.

hello@baronpublishing.com

ISBN: 979-8-9866772-0-0 (paperback)
ISBN: 979-8-9866772-1-7 (ebook)
ISBN: 979-8-9866772-2-4 (hardcover)
ISBN: 979-8-9866772-4-8 (audiobook)

Ordering Information:
Special discounts are available on quantity purchases by corporations, associations, and others. For details, contact hello@johngsamuel.com

TABLE OF CONTENTS

DON'T ASK THE BLIND GUY FOR DIRECTIONS

A 30,000-Mile Journey for Love, Confidence, and a Sense of Belonging

JOHN SAMUEL

FOREWORD

Dear Reader,

This book is about my journey to hell and back—but also what I found on the other side of it: the importance of accepting yourself, advocating for yourself, creating experiences that are accessible for everyone, and realizing what is possible when you feel as if you belong.

If you're reading this book, you've probably faced some challenge in your life that was out of your control, and you felt alone. The good news is that you don't have to go to hell and back to learn those things too.

I hope my journey shows you the power of accepting yourself for who you are, as well as accepting others for who they are—and shows you how to stop looking and start *seeing*.

CHAPTER ONE

HOME

The rain pounded down on my old white Jeep Grand Cherokee, banging against the metal frame and rattling the interior. The downpour was so loud I couldn't hear the music on the radio—I couldn't even hear myself think.

But if I could, I would be screaming.

I was driving down one of the narrow suburban streets of Cary, a suburb of Raleigh in North Carolina, the picturesque town I grew up in. When it wasn't being drowned in rain, Cary was the type of place where lawns are manicured to the perfect height and lush big green oaks dot the landscape. When my parents moved to Cary in 1980, there were fewer than 20,000 people living there, but as the low cost of living and good schools continued getting attention, people started coming in droves. Cary gained a reputation as the acronym CARY (Containment Area for Relocated Yankees) because it became rare to find someone who was actually from there.[1]

---

1   Asma Khalid, "Newcomers to U.S. South Mark Shift in Regional Politics," All Things Considered, NPR, August 11, 2016, https://www.npr.org/2016/08/11/489661947/newcomers-to-u-s-south-mark-shift-in-regional-politics.

I was, but people couldn't understand how someone born in Cary with a name like John Samuel could be a Brown kid like me.

Driving in Cary was hard enough for me on a normal day. My vision was rapidly declining for a reason I didn't understand yet, and I refused to tell anyone about it. I wanted to belong so badly that I didn't care what happened after I climbed into the driver's seat.

Now, as a 17-year-old, I had managed to work around my driving issues for the past year. I made sure to do most of my driving during the day, when I could see better. Details and signals were hazy, but I made sure to take the same routes on roads I knew well.

I tried to avoid driving at night, because it was especially tough. Everything got darker and darker, and it was harder and harder to see things—everything except lights. Lights were blinding. Think of yourself driving—if you glance at a passing car's high beams, you might have difficulty seeing the road for a second. For me, that moment would stretch for three or four seconds. I began wearing sunglasses at night when I drove—not to be cool or to mimic every singer from the 1980s, but because they helped to make the bright lights not so bright.

Even though I had learned how to get around my driving difficulties, nothing could help me on this one night. A torrential downpour was causing rain to cascade down my windshield like a waterfall, but with broken wipers, I had no way of seeing past it. I was holding a napkin in my free hand and clearing off my foggy windows every few minutes. And anytime I could see, I was blinded by the reflection of light in any puddle.

Things got worse when a car from one of the side streets turned left in front of me to enter the street I was on, the main road. Its headlights flooded the inside of my Jeep with light, forcing me to squint and guess where I was going.

I tried to keep my direction as straight as possible, but when the wheels on the left side of my car sunk in a puddle, my steering wheel got a mind of its own. Suddenly, I was swerving into the opposite lane, where the oncoming car was heading straight for me. The driver laid their hand on their horn and kept it there.

The sound pierced my ears and rang for an eternity. I held my breath and waited for the end.

Just when I thought my life was over, I felt my hands rise and grip tightly on the wheel. It was as if my instincts were taking over. I tugged the wheel back to the right and veered back into my lane again.

The car continued forward, its horn still blaring, but its sound grew quieter. Somehow, I was okay.

I clicked on my emergency lights and pulled over to the side of the road. My wheels were sinking into mud, but I didn't care. I needed time to catch my breath and let my heart calm down. When the reality of what had just happened sunk in—that I could've killed two people, one being me, all because I couldn't see—I burst into tears.

The tears streamed down my face like a river, forcing me to gasp for air as I drowned in my tears. The more I cried, the more confused and desperate I felt.

There was one question I kept coming back to: *What the hell is going on?*

Eye toward the Future

Growing up, I had a clear vision for the future.

I would become a business executive like my father. Go to a top-tier university and earn excellent grades. Climb the corporate ladder, own fancy suits, host business dinners, and drive a fancy European car with butter-soft leather seats. I was going to be *successful.*

Becoming a doctor or engineer seemed reasonable—that was the expectation anyway, as the son of Indian immigrants. My parents came to the U.S. from India in 1969, from the southwestern state of Kerala, where there is a large Christian population.[2] That's how I ended up with a name like John

---

2   "Christianity in Kerala," Kerala Tourism, accessed April 25, 2022, https://www.keralatourism. org/christianity/.

Samuel.

I grew up hearing about how my father came to the U.S. with $7 in his pocket, and how, after spending one of those dollars on a pack of cigarettes and 50 cents on a necktie, he was able to work his way through college while supporting his family back home in India. By the time he moved to North Carolina, he had already started his ascent from engineer to corporate executive despite landing in the country only a decade earlier with a little grasp of spoken English.

I admired his story. I wanted to be like him.

When my parents moved to the area, there were only five other families from Kerala, so we were a tight-knit group. On weekends, the families all would gather at one of our homes. The dads could be found sitting around a table playing cards, while the moms were in the kitchen blending spices for *biryani*, a savory baked rice-and-meat dish, or *sambar*, a vegetable-based stew. Meanwhile, we kids could be found playing basketball in the driveway. Despite being surrounded by this Indian community, I was the only Brown kid in my class up until seventh grade.

Just as I wasn't surrounded by many people growing up who looked like I did, I also didn't know anyone who had a disability.

According to the Centers for Disease Control and Prevention (CDC), 61 million people in the U.S., or 26% of the population, have a disability, and some experts estimate that nearly 20% of those impairments are considered to be invisible, meaning not immediately obvious to others.[3]

At that point, disability meant "handicapped," which I didn't realize at the time wasn't inclusive language, and I only associated that term with parking spots. The only exposure that I could recall was seeing one man

---

3   National Center on Birth Defects and Developmental Disabilities, "Disability Impacts All of Us Infographic," Centers for Disease Control and Prevention, March 8, 2019, https://www.cdc.gov/ncbddd/disabilityandhealth/infographic-disability-impacts-all.html#:~:text=61%20million%20adults%20in%20the.

walking around town with a cane in his hand—and he must've lived nearby because he would always pass by our car as we drove out of our neighborhood. He often wore a baseball cap and sunglasses with a button-down shirt and windbreaker. He stood out to me not only for the white cane but also for the fact that he was walking on the sidewalk of the main road—no one typically walked beyond our neighborhood streets. He looked friendly enough, but I felt sorry for him. I couldn't imagine the life of someone who's blind.

Blindness just wasn't something that crossed my mind. But that didn't matter—it was always waiting for me.

The first time I noticed something wasn't right with my eyesight was when I was about 10 years old at my cousin's house. My cousin was talking about the stars in the sky, so I scanned and squinted and scrunched my eyes, trying to get a glimpse of the pinpoints of light … but I couldn't really see them.

Every year when I returned to his house, my vision had become worse and worse until all I saw above was midnight blue, a sea of darkness.

And because I had very real vision issues but no way of accepting them, I struggled in school. I wasn't a bad kid; I just didn't apply myself—at least that's what I kept hearing.

It wasn't as if I didn't try to speak up. For instance, when music classes began in elementary school and I couldn't see my sheet music, I tried to tell my teacher. Instead, I heard snickering in the classroom in response—the other students thought I was joking.

Because of their reaction, my teacher assumed the same. "That's one way to get out of playing," she quipped, before continuing with her lesson.

Blackboards made things even more difficult. Whenever a teacher would use chalk, erase it, and then write on top, it would look like a big gray blob to me. I couldn't even guess an answer at that point. I'd try really hard whenever I was called on, but I would look dense, as usual.

At that point, I started relying on humor to get out of situations that would make me look bad. Sometimes, I would offer an outlandish answer to get some laughs from the other kids. Humor became a useful shield for me.

But it came at a price. Soon I was getting *C*s and *D*s, and my reputation as a class clown was spreading through the school—leaving my parents quite disappointed.

It didn't help that my sister Susan, who is almost six years older, was just about perfect when it came to my parents' standards. She earned a near 4.0 GPA in high school and college, went to medical school, and got into an Ivy League school for her residency—making my parents proud and setting their expectations for me sky high.

Thankfully, at school I had a good support system that didn't care what grades I was getting. My high school friends were some of the top students in our class—and unlike everyone else, they knew something was wrong with my eyesight (not because I told them; they just seemed to know)—so they wanted to help me out however they could. My friend Jon dedicated many hours to driving me around, while my other friend Sid was even willing to put himself on the line to bolster my grades.

We had sophomore-year English together, and because both of our last names started with the letter *S*, we sat next to each other in the back. Not only could I not see the blackboard, making class and tests even harder, but having to mark my answers on Scantron sheets, multiple-choice, fill-in-the-bubble forms, was truly another level of murder on my eyes.

For our first test of the year, the test packets flew backward toward me after passing through the hands of everyone in my row. Then came the Scantron forms, thin, flimsy sheets of paper that were covered in rows of blue circles—blue circles that I would have to fill out.

This isn't going to be good, I thought.

When the test started, I watched the seconds tick away on my watch. When it came time for me to answer my first question, I could barely make out a thing between the test and my Scantron sheet.

Soon, it was filled with smeared, smudged graphite, hesitation marks and signs of struggle, and erasures to try and clean the scene of the crime.

That was when Sid came to my rescue—or *tried* to. He scooted his answer sheet to the other side of his desk and lifted it slightly toward me. "*Psst*," he whispered quietly. Thankfully, only a head or two turned, but the teacher didn't notice.

I looked up from my test and saw what he was offering me. I strained my eyes trying to catch a glimpse of his answers, but I immediately knew there was no way I was going to be able to read them.

I nodded his way, giving him a sign of my gratitude, but then shook my head, as if to say, *Don't worry about it. I don't need it.*

He raised his eyebrows in surprise, thinking I was being such an honorable guy. Little did he know, I would have taken all the help I could get.

I continued stumbling my way through high school—literally, whenever I would trip on something I couldn't see, as well as metaphorically. My GPA was barely above a 2.0, an ugly mosaic of everything but *A*s.

After enough frustration and incorrect answers and "I don't knows," I got my eyes checked at an eyeglass retailer and vision center at the nearby mall. They ran me through a barrage of standard eye tests. I studied their circular illustrations, trying to find the numbers within them, and nearly fell out of my chair when they blew shots of air into my eyes. Nope, nothing wrong there, just tears at the corners of my air-blasted eyes.

I looked through a viewer to check my peripheral vision, but they couldn't find any issues with it either, which made sense to me. My peripheral vision was always pretty good—everything else was the problem.

Then it came time to pull the phoropter, that alien-looking device, in front of my eyes and check my vision in each eye. The objects in the viewer were made clearer or blurrier with a series of lenses.

"Is the object clearer here …" *click*, "or here?" the doctor would repeat, over and over again.

At the end of the appointment, the optometrist didn't have any answers for me. My sight was inconsistent, so like my classmates and teachers and parents, the doctor thought I was messing around too.

With no diagnosis and a bit of a reputation, I figured, *If that's how it's going to be, why not mess around a bit?*

I started drifting and began experimenting with drinking and smoking pot. I'd do stupid things, often to look cool in front of my friends or to get a laugh out of people. One time, when I was skipping class with a girl, we went to a grocery store to get candy (we were planning on smoking pot, and I used to get the munchies), so I put a bag of Sour Patch Kids in my pocket. An employee saw me and called the cops.

I ended up getting suspended from school.

My parents were *horrified*. The incident was just about the worst thing possible. While my sister was a star student and future *doctor*, I was cutting class and getting kicked out of school.

Everything culminated on a day when my senior-year English teacher, Ms. Fenton, had had enough. I was goofing off in the back of the classroom, like always, flipping one of those thick erasers on my desk over and over again. Ms. Fenton eyed me like a hawk as she paced back and forth in the front of the classroom.

"Class, why do you think Shakespeare—" *plop* went my eraser after it completed another successful flip. Ms. Fenton cleared her throat, then went on, trying to ignore me. "Why do you think Shakespeare has remained relevant all these …"

PLOP.

"John!" she snapped. "Can you please, for the love of God, stop that!"

The classroom fell eerily silent. I did too. No teacher had ever been so direct with me. "Sorry, Ms. Fenton," I murmured, feeling more uncomfortable than actually apologetic.

Ms. Fenton stared out the window for a moment, then shot her glare back at me—her eyes somehow more piercing than before. She sighed. "This is why you'll never amount to anything."

Everyone froze, paralyzed by shock. None of the 17- and 18-year-olds around me had ever heard a teacher say something like that to a student. Meanwhile, I was trying to hide the fact that my jaw had dropped to my desk.

I didn't move or speak the rest of the class. I was humiliated. Angry. Ashamed. My ego was in the gutter, alongside my GPA. I knew people would write me off, but how was I supposed to recover when someone who was supposed to help, nurture, and mentor me completely shut me down?

By my last year of high school, it was as if I had become a self-fulfilling prophecy. I had tried to ask for help, but because no one took me seriously, the less serious I became. Was the cycle just bound to continue?

Ms. Fenton's comment haunted me from that moment on. Her statement wasn't just an indictment on my present but on my future too.

Was I doomed to be a failure?

Meanwhile, all my friends were getting acceptance letters for their top-choice universities. One received a top scholarship at NC State—full ride, all expenses paid. Another friend got into every top school that he applied to.

Not me. I received rejection after rejection from my top picks.

I did receive one acceptance letter—Virginia Commonwealth University (VCU), the same university where my sister was attending med school. That proximity was helpful for me since my parents were going to relocate to India for work after I graduated from high school, and my buddies would be attending other colleges.

VCU it was, then—it had to be.

From Comfort to Peril

I was full of hope the first time I stepped onto VCU's campus as a freshman. I had visited the campus several times before to see my sister, and I thought the familiarity would be helpful for me and my vision. I recog-

19

nized Monroe Park in front of me, with its tall trees, weaving gray sidewalks, and the constant chatter of students walking through it. I could also make out parts of the engineering building, where I was going to be studying. That building—the newest addition on campus—had a distinct look with tall glass windows and steel beams.

After spending some time taking in the campus beyond the sights—the whir of the cars behind me, the birds chirping in Monroe Park, the electric energy that surrounded me—I was ready to begin my new life. VCU could be a fresh start for me, a chance to create a new reputation and apply myself.

I turned around to face my parents, who were standing in front of our car. I had my entire life packed into two suitcases beside me—one of them a bright yellow (I initially picked it because I liked the color, but the color also inadvertently helped with contrast)—and my sister had hers. I said goodbye to my mom first, whose tears I could feel on my face as we hugged, and then my dad.

To my surprise, when I went in for a hug, I felt drops of water trickle on my neck and shoulder. My dad was crying—for the first time.

"I'll see you soon, Dad," I said as I pulled away from him. I checked in with my sister, who nodded back at me. We were both ready to go.

My sister went left, toward her off-campus row house, while I went through Monroe Park for my dorm, but not without waving goodbye to my parents first. Still crying, they returned the gesture and then disappeared into the car—possibly not wanting the memory of them with tears on their faces to be burned into our memories. Too late.

Before I knew it, I was alone, now blanketed by trees and comforted by the silence of nature. Something about it felt nice. Sure, part of me wished I could be at a better school with my high school friends, but it was actually nice to be on my own. I felt a sense of independence.

The only problem, as always, was my eyesight.

Monroe Park was unusually dark, due to the fact that the heavy tarp of leaves was covering me and the park lights in shade. Navigating the trees and sidewalks and people—not to mention the gangs of squirrels that called the park home—was a challenge, and my shins were proof of that. By the time I made it to my dorm room, they were bloody and bruised from walking into trash cans and benches.

This'll be one hell of a first impression, I told myself.

As it turned out, I didn't need to make a first impression. During my first week of school, like many undergraduate students, I had a tough time making friends and didn't have a lot of interaction with other people. I was disappointed when I would hear my friends talk about their own college experiences—tailgates at football games, parties, and fun. VCU didn't have a football program, and this was years before the school's basketball program gained national fame.

The students in the dorm who lived on the same floor as mine hung out together, and I wasn't included. I came across as quiet and shy, and for a while, I was all by myself—people would go out and party, and I'd be left behind. People would be in the bathroom the next morning, hungover and talking about their night, whereas I'd have gone to bed at 8 p.m. because I hadn't known that people were going out.

Maybe that isolation was for the best, because my vision issues continued to worsen. My vision field featured a series of blind spots, and at night, I felt as if I were walking through a pitch-dark cave using a fading candle flickering at its end.

Since I couldn't see properly, I kept tripping over or walking into things. My shins were a constant watercolor of reds and purples, bruises and bleeding. Curbs and rocks were a struggle. Puddles were unavoidable. I remained as clumsy as ever.

The difficulty of walking a few blocks or crossing a park at night forced me to often skip my evening classes. I memorized when sunrise and sunset were every day so I could make sure to get home in time. I was like a farmer. After daylight savings time began in March, I'd call that "Johnny's time." The days were longer, and the additional amount of sunlight dictated my happiness, well-being, and outlook.

But Johnny's time couldn't come soon enough.

At VCU, when you got a 2.0 or lower, you got an academic warning. After three academic warnings, you got suspended. Three strikes and you're out. I flittered right around that 2.0 level. One semester I'd be above, the next I'd be below that 2.0 level.

New school, same problems.

I couldn't take it anymore. During a break in the school year, I'd had enough with my eyesight and decided to visit a specialist. Something was definitely wrong, and my life had become severely affected and restricted by my vision problems. Maybe they could give me some eye drops, or special glasses, or something that would help me.

Instead, the specialist gave me something called an ERG, or electroretinogram. It's like an EKG for your eyes. They essentially put these contacts with wires sticking out of them on your eyes, and flash lights in your eyes so they can count your rods and cones.[4]

I was sent home to wait for the test results. About a week later, my dad had sent me to our house to retrieve something on his behalf, since he was still living in India with my mom. It was there, when I was alone at the house and rifling through the drawers in his desk, that the fax machine suddenly came to life. I jumped at the sound of its whirring, but when I turned around, all I found was a harmless piece of paper. I strained my eyes to read the small gray text on the white paper.

It turned out to be a lot more damaging to my mental state than I could've ever imagined.

The fax was from the specialist, telling me I had something called retinitis pigmentosa. I looked it up and found out that retinitis pigmentosa, or RP, was a degenerative and genetic eye condition. Eventually my eyesight

---

4   "Electroretinography," Medline Plus, accessed April 28, 2022, https://medlineplus.gov/ency/article/003388.htm.

would worsen to the point of blindness.[5]

Blind.

That one word felt like a death sentence.

In an instant, my entire world came crumbling down as I spiraled down a Google rabbit hole. I had all the symptoms, like difficulty seeing at night, appearing clumsy, and a reduced vision field—yep, all of the above. I would probably have to read Braille because one day I would not be able to read anything on paper. I learned the disease is genetic,[6] and even more damning was the countdown looming over my head: my research said my vision could disappear entirely within a year.

According to the CDC, as of 2012, 4.2 million people in the United States aged 40 years and older suffer from uncorrectable vision impairment, 1.02 million of whom are blind; this number is predicted to more than double by 2050 to 8.96 million due to the increasing epidemics of diabetes and other chronic diseases and our rapidly aging U.S. population.[7]

The more I learned, the more horrible I felt. I felt as if my dreams were being ripped away from me. How can you be a business executive if you can't see? What career could I have? What woman would want to be with me? Where could I live if I couldn't drive?

There was no escaping the dilemma anymore. It all was becoming very, very real.

While I wallowed in the devastating news, my parents found out from the specialist, who called them directly. They reacted with anger—not only did they not want to know anything else about it, but they also refused to go back to the doctor. I think they were doing everything they could to avoid

---

5 "Retinitis Pigmentosa," National Eye Institute, accessed April 25, 2022, https://www.nei.nih.gov/learn-about-eye-health/eye-conditions-and-diseases/retinitis-pigmentosa.
6 "Retinitis Pigmentosa," National Eye Institute.
7 "Fast Facts about Vision Loss," Centers for Disease Control and Prevention, 2020, https://www.cdc.gov/visionhealth/basics/ced/fastfacts.htm.

the fact that RP is genetic. They couldn't accept the diagnosis, and they denied that something was wrong with my eyes.

As for me? I didn't want anyone else to know about my condition either. I wasn't ready to be vulnerable. I wasn't ready to let anyone see the true me; I wanted to belong, not be an "other." I was going to keep pretending everything was fine while maintaining my secret. Another mistake, as I'd realize years later, because ignoring my disability led to my biggest failures—but embracing it would contribute to my greatest triumphs.

During my journey, I learned how the world is systemically unequipped to set up people with disabilities for success, even though those with disabilities are some of the most capable people out there.

According to an NBC News article, up to 20% of public-school students are served under the Individuals with Disabilities Education Act, but only 7% of Asian Americans are, the lowest of any group.[8]

---

8   Victoria Namkung, "Why Asian American Kids Are Under-Diagnosed When It Comes to Learning Disabilities," NBC News, October 1, 2021, https://www.nbcnews.com/news/asian-america/asian-american-kids-are-diagnosed-comes-learning-disabilities-rcna2425.

CHAPTER TWO

167 MILES

I drove back to VCU from my parents' place that night and spent the two-hour trip flipping from radio station to radio station so I could keep the melodies consistent. I knew any break in music would open the floodgates until my thoughts became uncontrollable. Then it would be all about my diagnosis—the ticking time bomb—the thing that would ruin my life.

I turned the radio up, put the windows down, and tried to sing along to the Backstreet Boys as if I didn't have a care in the world. I wanted it that way, and at this point, I was willing to do whatever it took to do so.

The next thing I knew, I was using my fake ID to buy a 12-pack of beer from the 7-Eleven by VCU's campus. I had no plans and nowhere to drink, but I knew that I didn't want to be alone with myself—and if a can of beer (or more) could be my companion, I would take it.

Just as I was passing $10 to the store clerk, a wave of guys flooded into the store. They were all put together on the outside, with their pressed polo shirts, khaki pants, and white Adidas shell-toe sneakers, but I could smell the stench of alcohol they brought in with them. "Hey, man!" one of them said, placing an unstable hand on my back. "Are you coming on the crawl?"

Outside the store windows, I could make out a larger group of people, who were all huddling around a guy with a lit torch in his hand. I didn't know what "the crawl" was, but I guessed it had to be some kind of frat tradition. Without anything better to do, I turned toward the person behind me and said, "Yeah, why not?"

The first place we went was an underground party in the basement in one of the frats. The heat of dancing bodies against my face was the first sensation I got—then, there was the overwhelming smell of sweat. The music was next, rattling my ears, and then there was nothing. No lights, only darkness.

When I realized I couldn't see, the air suddenly grew thick and heavy. While I tried to navigate the room between heavy breaths, I thought about how *this* was my future. Darkness. Nothingness. I put my hands forward, reaching out so I could hold onto something, but it only made me think about how my hands were acting as a cane.

I could see it already: shuffling my way through a busy street with a cane in my hand. Pushing away people as they tried to help me or apologizing to the ones I knocked down. All they would see, and all I could see, was "the blind guy."

I kept my hands out, waving them back and forth, until I finally found a wall. I leaned my back against it and felt a sense of relief.

I ripped open my case of beer and cracked open a can. I lifted it to my lips and let the beer pour down my throat. It was cold, fizzy, and cheap tasting, but for some reason, my ease grew the more I drank it.

When I finished the can, I felt as if I could finally breathe again.

The next thing I knew, my case of beer had disappeared, and I found myself in the middle of the dance floor. People had opened up to let me spin away, and some of them were actually rooting me on, even though I didn't remember telling them my name.

I felt on top of the world. If I fell down, it wasn't because I couldn't see—I was just drunk. If I bumped into someone, I was just drunk. If the world outside of me was blurry, well … I was just drunk.

I had found a way to exist as myself again, even if it meant some people thought I had a drinking problem. To me, that was better than going blind.

The Escape

I started going out often, which meant my already suffering grades were getting worse. I tried not to care too much because the situation felt out of my control—the school didn't know I was struggling with my vision, and I didn't want to own up to it—so I focused on other things.

Near the end of my first year at VCU, I started dating Casey. I was sitting on her bed, waiting to take her out on our third date, kicking my feet against her bed frame. "So, where are we going?" she asked from around the corner. She was finishing her makeup in the bathroom.

"I was thinking the Italian place a few blocks down. Are you up for a little walk?" I joked, but irony had different plans for us. Like clockwork, it started pouring outside. "Oh, crap," I murmured.

"Did it just start raining?" she called back. "John, you can just drive us there, right?"

Uh, no way, I thought. "I have a flat tire, sorry!" It was a lie, but I was just scared.

Casey's roommate, Divya, who had been reading on her bed, sat up. "You can take mine, if you want."

Things were starting to get much more complicated. "That's okay …" *C'mon, think, John, think!* "We should just walk! It'll be romantic."

Divya's blank expression said it all: *This guy is ridiculous.* "I don't think Casey will think it's romantic, right, Casey?"

"Yeah, no thanks," Casey replied with a laugh. "John, why don't you just take Divya's car?" Casey knew I had a license.

I racked my brain trying to think of a different excuse. Since I was taking Casey out to dinner, I couldn't say I didn't have my license because I forgot my wallet. I could lie about having a few beers before our date, but that would just make me look bad. After running through a few more fruitless excuses, I realized I had nothing.

"I just can't. Sorry." I looked down at my feet as the room grew silent. I could feel Divya staring at me, and I knew Casey didn't know how to respond.

After a minute of awkwardness, Casey came out of the bathroom and tried to seem cheery. "I'll just drive. I want pasta too badly anyway." She shared a glance with her roommate, who was grimacing with confusion.

Still, I exhaled. Crisis averted—for now anyway.

We continued dating through the first part of the summer break. Long distance worked great until she asked me to come meet her and her family. She was in eastern Virginia, which meant a long and unfamiliar drive for me coming from Cary. Part of me also worried that the longer we dated, the more likely she was to figure out my visual impairment. I couldn't let that happen—I could barely make sense of it myself, so how was I going to make sense of it to another person?

I broke up with her over the phone the next day, telling her I wanted to be single during the summer while I was with all my friends back home. She was crying on the other end of the line, her voice cracking as she tried to understand why I was ending things. I kept it brief because I had to.

If we talked any longer, the pit would've kept growing in my stomach until it consumed me.

In Pursuit of Denial

By the start of my sophomore year, I had become known as a partier, but I still didn't have any close friends. Instead, I spent a lot of my spare time at the gym. One day, I was wearing an Enloe T-shirt, from the high school I went to in Raleigh, when another guy recognized the name. He told me he was from Eden, a small town in North Carolina, then invited me to his frat's party that night.

Pretty soon, Ankush and I became good friends. Later that semester, he encouraged me to rush for his frat in the spring, and even though I originally wasn't interested in the fraternity culture, it sounded like a nice way to make some friends and belong somewhere on campus. I told him I would, but my semester was about to go in a very different direction.

Denial became a good friend, and to my surprise, a friend to my family. Ever since my parents found out about my diagnosis, they had been obsessively searching for a cure or treatment.

They weren't alone in that effort, though. I was grieving in my own way, so I'd pray to God for a cure and ask him to "fix me"—even though I was never broken. Like my parents, I would also scour the internet for medical studies and miracle cures. I remember reading something about how, during World War II, British pilots in the Royal Air Force ate bilberry jam to improve their night vision.[9] I even went to Whole Foods to buy supplements and tried taking them. (Surprise, surprise—they didn't work.)

But in the spring of my sophomore year, my mom ended up coming to Richmond and staying at a hotel for about a month to give me this Ayurvedic herbal medicine. There was no cure for my eye condition, but in India, this medicine was supposed to help. It tasted terrible—it was a blend of herbs mixed with ghee—and I had to take it twice a day, in the morning and evening, and the medicine had to be consumed at the perfect temperature.

As horrible as the experience was, it meant a lot that my mother tried to help. Desperation was better than denial.

Desperation with Denial

Before long, I was starting my junior year at VCU, and I was finally ready to pledge Ankush's fraternity. The following semester, I would become a brother of the Alpha Kappa Lambda fraternity. For the first time at VCU, I felt as if I had found a group where I belonged.

But the feeling would be short lived.

My grades slipped below the 2.0 barrier again that fall. I already had two strikes—one more semester with a sub-2.0 GPA and my career at VCU would be over.

---

9   John Briley, "Findings of Fact," *The Washington Post,* June 6, 2000, https://www.washington-post.com/archive/lifestyle/wellness/2000/06/06/findings-of-fact/3ba372a1-18cb-4f4b-83f9-c0f-c021a604c/.

The end of the semester was coming up fast, so when I found out my GPA was in the danger zone, I went to all my professors asking them, pleading with them, begging, "Please just change my grade, whatever you can do." Because I was on the border, bumping up one letter grade—like a C to a C+—would keep me in school. But so far, no one would.

Finally, I went to my ethics professor's class. It was my last opportunity. I hoped that, maybe, because I had a B– in the class, I would have a better chance of getting my grade moved up. When I walked through the doors of his office, he was surprised to see me—and I couldn't blame him. I had never been to his office hours before the class. I was surprised he even knew my name. "John," he said, "is everything okay?"

With tears building in my eyes, I said with a sharp breath, "I really need your help." I explained the situation, how just one step up from a B– to a B would keep me at VCU, but I didn't go into my visual impairment. I still didn't want to say the words "retinitis pigmentosa" out loud, and I got the feeling that if I told him about my diagnosis, all he would say was "Why are you telling me this now?"

After my panicked explanation, my professor simply responded, "If it's only one grade you need, how come you didn't ask any other professor over the last three years to change one grade?"

Little did I know, I wasn't alone in my academic struggles.

> In 2016, of the students who identified as being blind or visually impaired, 22.3% didn't even graduate from high school, 31.6% received a high school diploma or GED, 30.3% had some college education or earned an associate degree, and only 15.7% received a college degree or higher.[10]

I left his office with my head down. There was nothing I could do now.

10   "Blindness Statistics," National Federation of the Blind, accessed April 25, 2022, https://nfb.org/resources/blindness-statistics.

I wanted to hide my limitations, but in doing so, I hid my abilities too. I kept failing and falling short, and everyone made assumptions: I was too aloof or too proud or too stupid or too clumsy. My high school English teacher's voice rang in my ears: *You are never going to amount to anything.* Was she right?

Denial Accomplished

When I returned home for winter break at the end of the semester, I knew I was getting *the letter*—the letter I couldn't avoid, the one on official letterhead that spelled out my fate in black text: *s-u-s-p-e-n-d-e-d*.

I had hoped that I was wrong and that one of my teachers would have had a change of heart, but then the letter arrived.

I took the letter and hid it under a pile of papers in one of my drawers. As time passed, the guilt grew in my stomach, like an emotional tapeworm, until it exploded on Christmas Day. We were sitting around the tree, the smell of pine permeating through my nose, enjoying each other's company and conversation. Then it came time for presents.

My mom placed a box on my lap with a big grin on her face. I quickly ripped away the sheets of thin paper until all that was left was a box. It was black, smooth, and heavy. I lifted up the top of it and couldn't believe what was inside.

A TAG Heuer watch. Its face was a shimmering blue, its band was made up of metal that was cold to the touch. I had been working every summer to save up for one, and now, here it was—the exact one I wanted. "For all your hard work these past few years," my mom added.

My smile slowly faded.

"What's wrong?" she asked. "Is it not the right one?"

"No, no!" I planted the smile back on my face and kept it there. "It's perfect. Thank you so much." I put it on my wrist and immediately felt the weight of it.

I spent the rest of the day with that smile planted on my face, not wanting to acknowledge or show what hid underneath it: a failure. An undeserving person. I mean, I had just been kicked out of college. What would I even need a fancy watch for now?

At the end of the day, I went up to my room and hid behind my closed door. I could finally breathe again, but when I did, the questions came flooding back in: *What do I do now? How am I going to get back into college?*

I sat down at my desk, buried my head in my hands, and let the tears run down my face. When I opened my eyes again, all I could see was my reflection in the glass on top of my desk. Looking at myself made me even more angry and confused. *What am I doing with my life? What's the point of anything?*

In a fit of rage, I slammed my fists down onto the desk. The glass shattered, and so did my reflection. Tiny pieces made it into my hands. The shards lay all around me. I froze.

A few seconds later, I heard my parents running up the stairs. If I didn't act quickly, they would know that something was wrong just by looking at my teary eyes. "Johnny, are you okay?" my dad called out.

"Yes!" I shouted back, trying to hide the fractures in my voice. "Everything's fine … I just knocked something over!"

But it wasn't enough to deter them. They didn't stop moving until their footsteps were outside my door. My mom started, "Are you sure—"

"Don't come in! There's glass everywhere." I held my breath.

After a few more seconds, some unsure shuffles, and possibly a shared glance between the two of them, my parents went back down the stairs. "Let us know if you need anything," said my dad, his voice fading. Still paralyzed with fear, I stared straight ahead of me and dared not to move in the pile of glass.

I knew I would have to tell them at some point—but not just yet.

After that night, I dove into a research frenzy. Failing out of college was unheard of in my parents' circle, so I was looking for any information that would lessen the blow for them. Eventually, and luckily, I stumbled onto

NC State University and its Lifelong Education program. There, I would be able to audit classes and earn credits in a flexible way, all without actually having to be accepted to the University. I would be able to take seven credits a semester, but summer was broken into two semesters, so that gave me an opportunity to take 28 credits in a calendar year, which was just two credits shy of a full-time student. One other (admittedly biased) factor was the fact that a lot of my high school friends were there too.

Finally, a few days before I was supposed to go back to VCU, and my parents back to India, I felt prepared enough to sit my parents down and share the news. There was a lot of screaming and disappointment, but ultimately, my parents encouraged me to apply for the NC State program.

The next day, I went to NC State and headed for the McKimmon Center. It was drizzly and gray out—so not the most optimistic-looking of days—but I went inside and took an application form.

I struggled to scan over the details: "students are only allowed to take seven credits at a time." I kept going until I reached the question "Have you ever been academically suspended from another university or institution?"

Um. This question was it for me—the kiss of death. But after grappling with what to do for a bit, I landed on just not checking the box.

Because of that blank box, I was sure I wouldn't get into the program. When two weeks passed and I got my decision back in the mail, I was shocked to find out that I was cleared to enter. It gave me a ton of relief, and I could quite literally feel the tension escape from my shoulders.

That notice also happened to be the first time I read the fine print of the program. I wasn't registering for classes with everyone else because I wasn't an actual student. I was simply taking whatever classes were available, and those often ended up being the first class or the last class of the day. There was always a reason why the classes weren't filled, so that first semester, I ended up taking seven credits—an accounting class, a gym class, and an economics class, all of which were general education requirements. Since I wasn't technically a transfer student, whatever credits I had gotten at VCU were now useless, so I was starting from scratch.

I also didn't tell Ankush right away that I wasn't coming back to VCU, so when my bedroom remained empty, he realized I wasn't coming back to Richmond. He, along with everyone else, assumed I had transferred to NC State to be back with my high school friends. I had curated that narrative a little bit, but the optics of the situation mattered to me. It did to my parents too.

And honestly, it seemed to work. Everything was falling into place, and I even ended my first semester at NC State with an A in my accounting class—my first college A. Because of that, I decided to go down the accounting route.

But eventually, things changed, as they always do. My friends graduated eighteen months after I started at NC State, so I ended up moving back home. At this point, it had been four years since my parents had moved to India for my dad's work, so they moved back home too. It was as if we were all returning at the same time.

With my friends gone, I wasn't going out—my life revolved around school and part-time work and home. I became lonely, and I missed my friends, but without anyone to hang out with, I poured myself into my studies.

Despite the fact that I would often have to leave class early because of the changing sunset time, my grades crept up, little by little. The circumstances—living at home, my friends off doing big things—lit a fire under me. I had to get my act together and keep it together. I still wanted to make something of my life, to prove the Ms. Fentons of the world wrong. I didn't want to be stuck forever, and yet, I couldn't shake the feeling that something was going to go wrong. It always did.

Fear of the Dark

I was waiting outside of my adviser's door for our afternoon appointment. At this point, I had been at NC State for four years and had accumulated enough credits to graduate. This was the moment of truth: when my adviser would tell me whether or not I could graduate this semester.

The TAG Heuer on my wrist ticked dangerously close to the hour. Staring at my watch, I wondered if my mom was going to be proud of me for finally graduating.

Mr. Cusak popped his head out of the office exactly at 3 p.m. He was wearing that same friendly smile he always had on, which made me think there was no way he was going to deliver any bad news to me now. "John! Come on in."

I took a seat inside his office. We had a meeting every semester, so I knew the space well, but there were so many things inside of it that I always found something new to notice. This time, it was the display of fountain pens in the back of the room.

After a bit of polite conversation, Mr. Cusak said, "Well, let's get into what you're here for, shall we?" He clicked around a few times on his computer, and after some silence, his face fell flat. "Oh."

"Oh? What's wrong?" I sat forward in my chair, thinking there was no way I had worked so hard for so many years at NC State just to have to do another semester.

He had trouble looking in my eyes. "I'm so sorry, John. They've decided to take you out of the program."

Everything went still and quiet, including me. "What do you mean? How is that possible?" The words came out of my mouth so feebly and small, as if I had already lost the fight before it had even begun.

"It seems that the admittance board found your records from VCU. It slipped through the cracks when you first applied."

"What? No …" I started to feel faint, and the world around me collapsed. The walls started to melt into the ground. The fountain pens bled black ink. My heart pulsed out of my chest. "This is … this is impossible."

My head grew heavier and heavier until I felt myself falling—and then there was no more. Just the world fading into nothing … blackness, and …

I sat up in my bed and gasped for air. My sheets were wet with sweat, and my body was cold. As reality started to settle in, my breathing slowed. The gentle morning sun drifted through my window and washed a wave of calmness over me. *I'm fine*, I told myself. *I'm fine.*

But when I checked the date and saw what time it was, I realized I was *not* fine. It was a big day, and I was running late.

I hopped in the shower, rinsed the nightmare off me, and tried to look as put together as I could in the shortest amount of time possible. Then I grabbed the red graduation cap and gown hanging in my closet. They felt so crisp and neat, falling around my shoulders for the first time.

When I got to campus, I joined my line for the ceremony inside historic Reynolds Coliseum—the old home of the Cardiac Pack, the name given to the 1983 NC State Wolfpack basketball team, whose Cinderella story shocked the nation and ended with a national championship.[11] It was winter and far too cold outside to be enjoying the typical sunny spring ceremony that I thought I would be participating in when my parents dropped me off on the VCU campus six and a half years earlier. Yet I took my seat in the back row of seats on the basketball court, of course, for *S*. After some long speeches from classmates I didn't know, our names started to get called. One by one, my row diminished until it was my turn to go.

When "John Samuel" was called, I made my way up to the stage, shook too many hands to count, and took the piece of paper that gave me a degree. As I stood on that stage and felt the lights flashing in my face, I couldn't help but smile. I had actually graduated from college.

I wasn't a traditional student in any way: I had earned my way until I was finally accepted in a full-time program. I didn't know anyone in my classes there, but after four years at NC State, I was officially a college graduate with a bachelor's degree in accounting—and just like the Cardiac Pack that was the most unlikely team to win the NCAA Championship, I might have been the unlikeliest member in my graduating class.

---

11   "Looking Back at the 'Cardiac Pack,'" NC State University Bulletin, April 4, 2008, https://projects.ncsu.edu/project/newsletter-int/archive/2008/04/04-02/1983-memories.php.

But what was maybe the most remarkable thing about my Cinderella story was the fact that I accomplished that goal without any of my professors or classmates understanding my visual impairment. If I could get a bachelor's degree while hiding my disability, maybe I could do the same in the working world. Maybe I could even become a business executive like my father, just as I envisioned when I was a boy.

No one needs to know the extent of my issues, I reassured myself. Instead, I decided right then and there that I was going to conceal my diagnosis as long as I could—maybe forever.

CHAPTER THREE

8,751 MILES

A burst of languages hit me like a slap in the face the first time I stepped out of the airport in India. There was Hindi, Kannada, Malayalam, Telugu, and Tamil and so many more dialects and languages that I didn't know, all of them yelling, "Taxi!" in some way or another. Stray dogs scuttered past me, their long nails clicking against the airport floor. Babies were crying all around me, while kids were scurrying by my feet. The smell of sweat, intensified by the heat, stung my nostrils.

As my taxi pulled closer into the city of Bangalore, I noticed the streets, crammed with cars, bikes, trucks, and rickshas, along with the overwhelming honking, which was consuming my ears. Everyone was shouting at each other and not getting anywhere. The heat was humid and thick outside my window, the air heavy like a wool coat.

There was a vibrancy to this place, but it was overwhelming—kind of like my senses were on fire.

Bangalore was supposed to be the Silicon Valley of India.[12] *Yeah*, I thought, *I can see that.* Out of my peripheral, I caught glimpses of tall towers, sleek offices, and people in suits walking down the street. We even passed the building of the tech company I was going to be working for, Sasken.

It felt as if I was finally back on track to accomplishing my dreams—and Bangalore was the key. I had been worried that my world in North Carolina wasn't arranged in a way that would guarantee long-term career success. There was too much driving involved, it felt too small and limiting, and I had that reputation for not taking anything seriously.

If I had stayed in North Carolina, I figured my disability would eventually become apparent and destroy my career prospects. And in order for me to achieve my dream of becoming a business executive, I needed to keep my reality subdued and hidden away—or at least that's what I believed at the time.

2021 data from the U.S. Bureau of Labor Statistics shows the rate of unemployment at 10.1% for people with disabilities, compared to 5.0% unemployment for people without disabilities.[13]

I started looking abroad instead and weighed my options: in a place like China or India, I would make less money than in the U.S., but I would be able to afford a driver, which was necessary at this point. I narrowed it down further to India, where my parents already had two cars and said they would cover the cost of a flat for me—meaning my main expenses would be gas money and paying the driver. My dad also had some high-level connections there, which would make finding a job a lot easier.

In India, maybe my experience abroad could become the main focus of my résumé, instead of my education. I could shape my narrative that way.

---

12   Saritha Rai, "Is the Next Silicon Valley Taking Root in Bangalore?," *New York Times,* March 20, 2006, https://www.nytimes.com/2006/03/20/business/worldbusiness/is-the-next-silicon-valley-taking-root-in-bangalore.html.

13

That was how I found Sasken. Now everything was falling into place.

While I was excited to be somewhere new and different, I also knew I'd have to be as careful as ever in India. If anyone got a whiff of my sight impairment, they would be able to take advantage of me.

My disadvantage became especially challenging when I was looking for a driver. I needed to have a guardian angel more than a driver because I had to be the most vulnerable with them. Even if I didn't tell a driver about my eyesight, they would be able to tell something was off and could easily take advantage of me.

Finding the right driver turned out to be a job within itself. Manjunad, who had been a driver for my parents when they lived there a few years earlier, helped connect me with one young driver. I tried to bond with him by sitting in the passenger seat, but he then felt too comfortable with me and didn't take his job seriously. After that, I had to start searching again.

Manjunad connected me with a second driver, but this time, I wasn't going to make the same mistake again by getting too comfortable and allowing him to push the boundaries like the previous guy. I decided to sit in the back seat to keep some distance and maintain a strictly professional relationship, but this driver kept prying and asking me all of these personal questions about my finances, so he didn't work out either.

When I came out of work one night, there was Murgon waiting for me, another contact from Manjunad. He carried a lot of hair on his head— enough to match his big smile. I wasn't sure we were going to be a good match—Murgon didn't speak a lot of English, and I probably had more in common with the other drivers because we were closer in age—but I still hopped in the car, deciding to try him out anyway.

He drove me to a restaurant after work, where I had plans to meet a colleague for dinner. After getting out of the car, I stepped onto the sidewalk and started heading toward the restaurant. In India, the sidewalks are made up of tiles of concrete instead of being one consistent stretch as they are in the States, and oftentimes, hiding underneath them, is a large gap and then sewage.

That's right: sewage. Sometimes, you could even smell it.

I gingerly treaded across the tiles alone in the dark, knowing the restaurant was only steps farther. I took another step forward with confidence, but this time, there was nothing beneath my foot. No sidewalk. Just air.

My foot was sinking down into the nothingness, and there was nothing I could do about it—except panic.

Just as I was about to open my mouth to scream, I felt a hand take hold of my back, and then another slip around one of my shoulders. "I've got you," was mumbled in poor English into my ear. It was Murgon.

He had been forewarned that I had a problem seeing, but he didn't know how severe it was. Even so, he had stayed by my side the whole time and saved me from falling before I even knew what was happening. Murgon had never left my side, even though I thought he had, and from that moment on, he never would. He became my guardian angel, and without him, getting around in India alone while going blind would have been pretty much impossible.

I quickly learned how important it was to have someone like Murgon everywhere I went. Allies could make the difference between safety and danger, maybe even life and death.

Murgon's main job was to take me to and from work at Sasken, a communication software company, where I was a corporate functions analyst. The building looked like a hotel, with balconies rising seven floors up from a courtyard full of grass and pretty trees. My desk was located in the finance and accounting department wing, which was located on the ground floor.

The typical workday started much later than I was accustomed to in the U.S., with most people getting to the office after 9:30 a.m., so there were only a few hours between the start of the workday and lunch. There was a cafeteria, better known as the canteen, which served hot food throughout the day.

Along the way over there for lunch one day, I was already thinking about a veggie grilled cheese masterpiece when a group of guys in pressed white shirts and dark slacks gestured my way. "Hey, American kid!" one of them called out. "Come here!"

I tried to hide my confusion and put on my most confident poker face as I pranced up to them. "Yeah?"

"How are you liking the new job?" asked the one standing in the front, tall and broad.

"It's great," I replied cheerily. "Nothin' to complain about."

"—yet," one of them interjected.

What? I wanted him to explain what he meant, but the conversation moved on too quickly. His comment came and went like the wind, and the tall one in the front took over again. "Why don't you eat with us?"

"Shrinivas, are you serious? C'mon, he's as American as they come. A hint of pepper would probably kill him."

"Okay, okay," Shrinivas said. "I'm just being cordial, Narayan."

We went to the cafeteria and, without thinking, ordered the spiciest Indian food off the menu. I didn't even like Indian food, but I felt the need to prove myself—and it seemed to work. They were all surprised when I plopped down my bowl of *bisi bele bhaat,* a local dish of rice, lentils, and vegetables that was as popular as it was spicy.

They watched in awe, simultaneously shocked and impressed, as I fed myself spoonful after spoonful of *bisi bele bhaat.* Meanwhile, it felt as if my eyes were bulging out of my head and my stomach was in the sixth circle of hell—but luckily, I could hide these things. I couldn't hide the perspiration building up on my forehead or the pain that was written all over my face.

Even though I was a dripping mess that day, I started eating lunch with the same group every week. We became great friends—and over time I eventually started to crave Indian food.

Out from the Shadows

Once I understood the lay of the land at Sasken, I sunk into my role there comfortably. The workplace environment was full of start-up energy, but not in the same way I was accustomed to back home. People weren't skateboarding around the office or sleeping in a nap pod on breaks; they were in neatly pressed shirts and pants—overly professional, even rigid.

I preferred the started-in-a-garage roots, so it was difficult to adjust my expectations when I first got there.

While I sought out the shadows, another challenge came from my peers and their perception of me. When I was first brought on, I was reporting to this rising star in the company—an Excel genius. (I'm terrible at Excel because the sheets are so hard for me to see.) He ended up leaving a few weeks after I arrived, so I was immediately thrust into his role—stuck with planning and managing the budgets for the IT, HR, Quality, Finance, and Facility Management departments.

Because I had hidden the truth about my eyesight from my coworkers and bosses, I was tasked with big responsibilities that shouldn't have been on my plate after only two or three weeks on the job. I was at a great disadvantage.

Technology upgrades could make the work more manageable, so I requested a laptop. With a laptop, I could position myself closer to the screen, which would mean less strain for my eyes compared to the big, bulky computer monitors in the office. I was given a laptop, but it came with unforeseen consequences. People started to suspect I was benefiting from some form of favoritism or nepotism.

Their suspicions were eventually confirmed, even though favoritism wasn't the reason they gave me the laptop. An email went out to the entire company, an announcement that read, "Joseph Samuel will be taking over as co–COO." My father.

One by one, everyone around me started popping their heads up from their cubicles and staring at me. My face went hot. I wanted to hide under my desk or bury my head in the tiny metal trash can by my foot.

My dad was only at Sasken for a few months because he got sick with cancer, but that didn't change the impression everyone got of me. In fact, it made things much, much worse.

Middle managers were particularly resentful because I was connected to *their* bosses. They would talk in their local language, point at me and laugh, or yell at me in the office. When a spurt of U.S employees joined after me, it was suddenly my fault. And because I knew senior management from my father, if the middle managers got in trouble with higher-ups, it was also my fault.

I found myself crying in the office, calling my mom and desperately asking, "What am I doing here?" The culture was awful. It eroded my already delicate self-esteem. The bullying got so bad that, one day, I was unexpectedly moved to the opposite side of the building, which was barely populated. I hadn't asked for the repositioning, but I guess enough people were tired of hearing the yelling at one whom senior management had brought in.

Even though the abuse was intense, it did cause me to make an important vow to myself: when I moved up in the world someday, I was never going to treat someone as I was being treated.

Curing the Ill

When my mom initially proposed I go to a retreat for my retinitis pigmentosa, I was interested. After all, I had invested quite a bit of time in yoga and meditation ever since I had moved to India because I heard they could benefit my eyes, and I had been dealing with a lot of stress from work lately.

A retreat sounded relaxing, and it came with an added bonus of a real—albeit, unlikely—cure, so why not try it?

The Ayurvedic retreat was many miles beyond civilization. The bustling city of Bangalore was behind me now, suddenly replaced with swaying trees, chirping birds, crisp air, and dirt underneath my brown loafers.

The retreat's campus was rustic—comprised of bare-bones architecture and one-story buildings that looked as if they were struggling to stand up straight. Scattered around the location were a few employees, all wearing the same modest, neutral-tone uniforms. All of them kept their heads down as I walked past them toward the check-in.

The woman at the front desk spoke with a Zen tone—and it was pleasant to the ears but also too fraudulent to be reassuring. She gave me a new set of clothes, gave me my room number, and showed me to the restroom. "You can change in here," she told me.

I took off my once-white polo, which was now stained beige from dust and sweat, and put on the long rags they gave me instead. They were a rough material, almost like a feed bag, which scratched my legs and arms. *This place really took rustic to a whole new level*, I quipped to myself.

Next were the shoes. I slipped off my leather loafers and stepped onto the cool stone floor. But after being alarmed by the feeling of something wiry underneath my feet, I rubbed one of my palms against the sole of my foot and found several pieces of hair on it. *Ew*, I thought, and clapped my hands together to get them off.

Just as I was slipping my second shoe off, there was a knock on the door. "Come in," I said. When the door opened, I recognized that it was the woman who had checked me in, but I was surprised to see clippers in her hands. "Uh, what are you doing with those?" I asked.

"Please sit down over there, in the back. It's to help with the treatment."

Oh, no … the hair on the ground. I made the connection as I shuffled toward the empty chair at the end of the room. She turned on the clippers and pressed the cold, spikey metal against my scalp. *Well, good thing I'm not too attached to my hair. If I can see again after this, it'll be worth it,* I considered.

When she finished shaving my head and took the rest of my items from me, I glanced in the bathroom mirror. I was unrecognizable. Blank, even. Just a man with retinitis pigmentosa.

I was led to my room soon after my haircut was finished, with nothing but an iPod in my hands. It was the only thing I was allowed to keep because, unlike my cell phone, it didn't give me any connection to the outside world.

I tried to settle into my room after realizing it was where I was going to spend the next three weeks. The place was dark and musty smelling. There was a towel on a rock-hard twin bed. And in the corner was a single chair, and against the opposite wall, a couch with a table in front of it. It was too dark for me to make out exactly what each piece looked like, but I could feel a bland, rough material on some of the items. No patterns or design. Lifeless and uncomfortable, like my clothes.

I kneeled down by one of the walls and felt around. The wall was chilled and hard, and so was the floor. *Concrete*, I realized. No metal spoon could get me out of this place.

All that was left to do now was wait for further instructions. I sat down on the bed and turned on my iPod, perpetually dragging my finger around the circular button because doing so was more interesting than my other options. When I lifted my finger up, I saw that I had landed on Kanye's "Jesus Walks," one of my favorite songs. I put my earbuds in and listened on repeat.

I spent about 90% of the rest of that day in that empty, soulless room. For lunch, they dropped a bowl of bland rice porridge called *congee* outside my door, and in the afternoon, it was time for treatment. They led me to a building not too far away from my room, where I was instructed to lie down with my chest up. It was also too dark to see, but I could smell a copious amount of coconut oil, and a pleasant mixture of cloves, cinnamon, and turmeric.

Before I could ask what was going to happen next, two clay cups, full of some liquid, were molded around my eyes. "What are you—" I tried to ask, but the liquid ran down to my mouth and gurgled inside of it before I could finish my question. My eyes stung so intensely that I wanted to scream and cry. I tried to lift my hands to pull the cups off, but another pair of hands held them down and shushed me.

How was this a retreat? It felt more like torture.

I rubbed my eyes when I was back in my room and looked around. Nothing looked or felt different. There was no change in my eyesight—just a change in me: I was now defeated and violated.

Before they had let me back into my room, they gave me my cell phone and told me I had five minutes to talk to whomever I wanted to. I dialed my mom's number.

"Johnny?" she said, on the other end of the line. "How is it going?"

I slumped onto my bed. "Honestly, I don't know. This place is … terrible. The treatment hurts, and I'm locked up in my room all day with nothing to do."

"Johnny, have faith in God and his plan. Believe that this could be worth it." And by "worth it," she meant that my eyes would be "fixed." We were both willing to do whatever it took for a cure. At this point, I figured any pain was worth it if it could change my reality.

"Okay. I'll try."

This cycle repeated every day for the next three weeks: rice porridge for breakfast, lunch, and dinner, treatment in the afternoon, and one phone call afterward. I stayed in the retreat the entire time—part of me was holding out hope that my miracle would come on the 21st day—but I was also making use of the time. I practiced mindfulness and thought about my life, my dreams, and my current position at Sasken.

As time progressed, it dawned on me that Sasken, and India, wasn't what I thought it would be. I had hoped I would feel a sense of belonging here, but I was more miserable than ever.

I left the retreat with the same eyesight but a new direction: I was ready to leave India.

Back at Sasken, I "saw" things differently. The other side of Sasken was quieter. It was an annexed branch that Sasken was planning on expanding into, but at the moment, there were only six other people in there. The peace was nice, but it removed me from the action of the office, which felt like a punishment. I was essentially taken out of the equation, and rather than middle management having to face consequences for their bad behavior, I suffered the consequences for them.

I tried to hold out at Sasken for a bit longer, just until I could plan my next move, but the abuse from my boss became too much. Even though I was in an annexed area, he would still seek me out to get in a screaming session here and there. It was as if I was his verbal punching bag.

Just after I turned my resignation in, I ran into him on his side of the building. "Watch out, John," he said, as he "accidentally" bumped into me.

Usually, I would just put my head down and continue forward—but not this time. I turned to face him, with my chin high and jaw tight, and said, "If you're going to talk to me like this, we should go into a conference room."

My boss stumbled backward, as if my words had knocked him off his feet. He opened his mouth to reply, but nothing came out, so I walked away instead. It felt as if I had just conquered some demon, or at least gotten a semblance of my dignity back.

No Safe Place?

I considered a number of possible destinations for my return to the United States. If I moved back to North Carolina, I would probably move back in with my parents—which wasn't ideal. On the other hand, my good friend Ankush, the one I had met at VCU, was going to grad school at New York University (NYU) and offered me a couch at his place until I got my bearings and found a job in the city.

I had always dreamed of living in New York City at some point in my life, so it felt as if I was being called there by the universe or … something not as cheesy. The city felt larger than life and full of opportunity—the perfect place for a young professional to move up in the world.

Beyond aspirational visions, I had heard New York was a practical place for blind people. Major metropolises have the benefit of robust public transportation networks, and because people there usually don't drive, you can just hop on the subway or hail a cab. Instead of having one Murgon, my driver, I could have lots of Murgons in bright-yellow vehicles, available whenever and wherever I needed them with the wave of a hand.

So, on a gray and rainy spring day, I flew from Bangalore to London and London to New York City, a 20-hour trip that takes you backward in time due to the time zone changes.

At the same time, I also felt as if my life was going backward. I was 26, going on 27, without anything concrete in my life. My friends were finishing grad school, getting married, and lining up great jobs, and I was effectively back at square one again, trying to establish myself while crashing at my friend's place.

After waiting out my layover in London, I got in line for my next flight to New York, where a woman with a toddler and a newborn baby was trying to cart around eight suitcases at once. She asked for my help, so I added my bag to her pile and struggled to push them through the terminal. Later on, it just so happened that she was sitting near me on the flight, so I helped shove those eight bags into the overhead compartments.

After seven hours passed, which included a few hours of dozing, we were finally nearing the end of our flight. Immigration card in hand, I turned to the woman beside me with the intention of asking for her help, hoping she was able to return all the help I had given her earlier. But just as I was about to open my mouth, she cut me off with a question of her own: "Hey, I'm sorry to ask for your help again, but could you fill out my immigration card?"

You've got to be kidding me, I thought. Instead, I said, "About that—"

"It's okay. I know. It doesn't have to be perfect."

Okay then. I took her card and hunched over it, squinting my eyes to try and make out the letters. It was too dark to see anything at all, so I clicked on the overhead light. When I did, the card immediately became washed out in white. Unfortunately, the dark alternative wasn't much better, so I left the light on and scribbled erratically as she passed off her information to me.

Throughout this process, the woman was trying to contain her two-year-old's outbreaks by holding onto him tightly. I heard him yell at her a few times and groan from inside her arms.

"Stop! Stop!" he cried, clearly on the verge of breaking free.

"Please be quiet," she whispered to him. "People are sleeping!"

"I don't care!"

Suddenly, the woman yelped in pain, and I heard her child's footsteps as he disappeared down the aisle.

"Take care of your son!" someone yelled at me from a few seats back.

I wanted to yell back at my fellow passenger, *That's not my son! I don't even know these people!* But I kept the thought to myself. This woman already had enough on her hands.

"Ouch, he bit me." She winced. "I'm so sorry. I'll be right back." Soon, she was gone too.

When she returned, she wasn't alone. Her child was in her arms again, faintly crying.

Thankfully, her toddler stopped crying when it came time for our landing, and I was able to garner a moment of peace again before helping the woman all the way through the baggage claim. When she finally had all of her bags, and I had my yellow suitcase, she left with her husband and brother.

An older woman whom I recognized from the flight came up to me after they walked away. "I saw everything you did for them. You're a very sweet boy, and God's going to bless you," she said. It didn't always feel that way for me, but it was a message I needed to hear.

Finally out of the airport, and as a cab took me closer to the city and the lights of the skyline shone faintly in the distance, I recalled the last time I had visited New York. When I was still living in North Carolina before going to India, I visited Ankush for his brother's 30th birthday party. Some of my high school friends were also in NYC at the time, so they told us

51

to come meet them at another party. I jumped in so many cabs that night and got around without a problem. The city's layout was so organized and simple, but it was big and beautiful too. Everything was just so ... *easy.*

More than anything, I hoped that it would be the same way for me. For once, I just wanted something to be easy—to get some relief and catch my breath for a moment or two ... to be able to do something on my own.

That choice was my best chance to succeed back in the States. New York, I thought, was finally going to be *the place* for me.

CHAPTER FOUR

17,052 MILES

New York City! A melting pot of dreams and dreamers, cultures and innovations, successes and struggles.

I gave the taxi what I thought was Ankush's address—125th and 11th—but it was actually 125 East 11th Street. After taking me about five miles farther uptown to Harlem, I pleaded with the driver to take me back to the village. On the way back down, I thought about how much I missed Murgon, my driver in India.

I was eventually able to reach Ankush's place, which was set inside a modest brick apartment building, also occupied by the nightclub Webster Hall. It blended in with the rest of the village, with handlebar-mustache hipsters passing by in front of it and too many cheese shops around to count. Ankush and I reunited on the sidewalk, where he grabbed my yellow suitcase and led me up the fourth-floor walk-up. Inside, he introduced me to his roommates, Mike and Yasmin, and the couch where I'd be living for free (in exchange for cooking and cleaning).

It wasn't a long-term solution, and it wasn't glamorous, but I needed to get my bearings. Plus, it was nice to be with Ankush again.

Soon after arriving in New York, I was able to get a job with the New York City Mayor's Office of Labor Relations through a family friend. I was so excited to start work, partially because I needed steady income, but also because I wanted to *make it*—and make it *here*. After losing a lot of my confidence from the work environment in India, I was hoping that the seemingly endless opportunities in New York would get me back on my feet. The accessibility was also exciting here. Between taxi cabs, subways, and buses, my transportation worries were largely manageable.

But on my first day of work, I quickly learned a different story. I combed my hair and picked out my nicest suit and tie because I wanted to make a good first impression, to look people in the eye and give them a smile, to shake their hands, to say the right things, and to find my groove.

And yet, the second I opened the cab door, I was overwhelmed by the chattering people, the quick pace of life, and the mixture of smells coming from everyone's to-go breakfasts. I hesitatingly joined the flow of the crowds, but just as I started to catch up to their speed, I felt my foot give way beneath me, just as it did in India, except this time, there was no Murgon to save me—just a sea of faceless, emotionless strangers who probably didn't blink once at the sight of my going down.

You see, New York's sidewalks often feature metal cellar doors built into them that, when closed, sit flat and are easy to walk over. One of these doors must've been open, and I didn't see it and lost my footing—but it didn't end there. I stumbled sideways and felt myself contort until I was upside down, somersaulting into an open stairwell. I screamed, "Ahhhh!" as my arms banged against the railway, my back realigned itself against the hard stairs, and my suit was ripped apart by the fall.

When the tumbling stopped, I stayed on the floor for a few moments to catch my breath. My head was spinning and everything in my body ached. "This can't be happening," I whispered as I raised my hands to assess them. They were cut and bloody, as if I had just been juggling knives.

There went my first impression. My first day on the job, and I was John Samuel, the guy who walked straight out of a horror movie.

That day, I realized that navigating New York wasn't going to be as easy as I thought it would be. At this point, the blind spots in my vision had come to resemble a doughnut, with a distorted but visible area in the center surrounded by a gap in my sight field. If I swiped my hand in front of me, I'd see it at some points and not at others. I could see clearest out of my peripherals—the edges of my field of vision outside of the doughnut were the sharpest and clearest. As a result, I would have to constantly crook my head this way and that, looking out of the sides of my eyes to place where I was. All of this would make New York very difficult to traverse.

Even though my New York fantasy was rapidly crumbling, I continued forward to my new job and encountered many obstacles along the way. My shoe would find its way into dirty, mucky water in the gutters, causing them to gain a few pounds and squish against the sidewalk. I had to push my way through scaffolding pipes, rising from the sidewalk like weeds, and find my way around some orange barriers that were randomly blocking streets.

I tried trailing my hand along the sides of buildings as I walked, but the city relies on lots of standpipes—two-pronged metal obstructions jutting out of buildings—for water, which happened to be located directly at shin level for me. I was back to having bloody shins like I did in college, which only worsened the mess that existed everywhere else on my body: the disheveled hair, the aching bones, the bloody hands.

By the time I had reached the office, I felt like collapsing. People swarmed around me, confused about my state, but all I could say between panting breaths was: "I'm John—John Samuel, the new outreach representative," before I got some water and cleaned up.

New York had literally left its mark on me—branding my body in wounds and scars. One thing I did learn that day, though, was that New York was not going to adapt to me: I had to adapt to it.

Adaptation 101

My job as an outreach representative took me to all five boroughs: Manhattan, Brooklyn, Queens, the Bronx, and Staten Island. I was to help city employees sign up for a tax-advantage deferred-compensation retirement program, called a 457 Plan.[14] During the recession, when people were mostly taking out their money, we were trying to educate them to keep their money in: typically, the best time to invest and stay invested is when the market goes down, after all.

I quickly learned that I needed to get licensed for this job. When I first got it, I was making $19 an hour—which was very hard to live on in New York, where my rent was $1,700 a month—but passing the Series 6 & 63 exams would make me licensed and bump me to $27, which still wasn't very much to be able to live on in NYC, but it was a huge increase from the $500 a month I was making in Bangalore. I received books to study for my licensing tests, as well as audio CDs. I still wasn't telling anyone that I couldn't see, and my worsening vision was making it harder and harder to read the words in the books.

With the books being so difficult to read, the CDs represented a lifeline as an alternative way for me to learn. I could pop a disc into my CD player, push Play, and listen to the information piping through my headphones. As words on the page turned blurrier, I could still devour books and soak up information not through my eyes but through my ears.

With all of my studying done, it came time to take the exam. I knew it was normally taken on the computer, and I wasn't sure if I would be able to take the exam that way, so I reached out for large-print accommodations, which was granted.

After putting my personal items in a locker, I was given three (sharpened) No. 2 pencils, a calculator, and a big eraser: I knew I was going to have to use it, after all.

I was then guided into a sterile-looking classroom with the type of fluo-

---

14   Daniel Liberto, "457 Plan," Investopedia, December 15, 2021, https://www.investopedia.com/terms/1/457plan.asp.

rescent lights that burn your eyes, and I was given my test in the back of the room. My eyes went wide with shock when I saw what the proctor was bringing to me: not a stack of normal-size papers, but a stack of *huge* papers, the size of a newspaper.

To my horror, the proctor plopped the papers on my test and walked away—leaving me speechless. I struggled to get my pleas out, "Er—wait—" but the fear had already taken over. I coiled back into my body uncomfortably and glanced at the pages in front of me, wanting to assess the damage. The pit in my stomach grew as I stared at the page and realized that the text was way too big.

This accommodation was not what I needed and made it worse than the normal testing method. Because my sporadic blind spots resembled a doughnut, and I had a much narrower visual field, it was harder to see bigger things because I would have to scan my head all over the place. These adjustments weren't very helpful, especially when accommodations are supposed to remove barriers, sometimes even being referred to as "productivity enhancers." At the time, I didn't understand how to advocate for myself, so I ended up straining and struggling, scanning my head at all different angles to properly read the questions.

Looking back, I realize I should've asked for better accommodation—but they should've also asked me what I needed instead of assuming. Accommodation can only work if both parties are equally invested—and usually, you can count on the person with a disability to be invested because they have to be. *It's their life.*

> As reported in a Job Accommodation Network survey, "most employers report no cost or low cost for accommodating employees with disabilities. Of the 1,029 employers who were able to provide cost information related to accommodations they had provided, 571 (56%) said the accommodations needed by their employee cost absolutely nothing. Another 403 (39%) experienced a one-time cost. Only 46 (4%) said the accommodation resulted in an ongoing, annual cost to the company, and 9 (1%) said the accommodation required a combination of one-time and annual costs. Of those accommodations that did have a one-time cost, the median one-time expenditure as reported was $500."[15]

Thankfully, even without proper accommodation, I still passed the exams.

Passing was the boost I needed in several ways, including being able to move to a new place. The day after Thanksgiving, I was sitting in our newly converted three-bedroom apartment with Ankush on the floor in the living room, on top of Japanese tatami mats. We had been living in this apartment for three months now with our other roommate, Javier, on 3rd Avenue and 11th Street, right around the corner from Ankush's old apartment above Webster Hall. After adding a wall to account for all of us, the place was a steal: It was in a newly renovated building, we basically had the fourth floor to ourselves, and everything was beautiful. Javier owned an art gallery, so we had lots of art hanging on the wall—including a print of James Brown, plus a black-and-white print of a guy wearing aviator sunglasses with a gold tooth in his mouth, which was the only color. The coffee table between Ankush and me was a fossilized fish bone in a stone slab, and even the plastic chair in the corner was made by some famous designer.

The place was great, but it was also 2008, and we had no money to afford anything else. We were eating oatmeal for every meal and still barely scraping by.

---

15   "Benefits and Costs of Accommodation," JAN: Job Accommodation Network, updated October 21, 2020, https://askjan.org/topics/costs.cfm.

"Hey!" Javier yelled in his Colombian accent, as he shoved through the door with grocery bags in his hands.

"What's in those bags?" Ankush asked.

"You'll be surprised, that's for sure." Javier set down the bags on our stone countertops, and they landed with a *thump*.

"It better not be a dead body," I joked as I ran to his side.

Javier then carefully pulled out turkey leg after turkey leg from the bags until the smell of raw meat filled the apartment.

"I got them from Whole Foods," Javier explained. "Post-Thanksgiving blowout, I guess."

We laughed at the absurd amount of meat on our counter and clinked a few legs together in celebration, as if they were champagne glasses.

That night, we put the turkey into water and boiled it, which made enough turkey broth to last us for months.

"What should we save it in?" I asked.

Ankush replied with a pile of leftover red Solo cups. "That works, I guess."

We poured the soup into all of the cups and froze them, and it became dinner for the time being.

"Recession soup," Javier quipped.

It is something I think about every November, and it brings a smile to my face.

NYC Overload

We spent a lot of time going out in New York—because after all, it was New York! One of the first groups I was introduced to there was Ankush's grad school friends, who'd want to go to fancy, overpriced clubs that I wasn't familiar with and left me with sensory overload. I also wasn't able to afford their lifestyle, so I always felt like a burden to them. I wanted to build deeper connections, to dig below the surface, and have true friends, people like Ankush, who would stick by me no matter what. I had learned how important allies were in high school and India.

Eventually, Ankush and I built a group that consisted of Ankush and me, Yasmin and Mike (Ankush's roommates when I first moved to the city), Mike's girlfriend Marina, Natasha, and two French women named Nono and Alice. We were like a modern-day cast of the TV show *Friends*, if Joey and Phoebe were Indian. We would often pregame by drinking and dancing in Mike and Yasmin's apartment before going out to dance at lounges and bars in the neighborhood. We loved to dance!

I opened up about my vision to only that close group of friends. We never put a name on it—not retinitis pigmentosa, not blindness, just "I can't see very well," but they could recognize my struggling, especially at night, so they would put their arms through my arms when we walked and helped me navigate in the darkness.

Other people weren't as kind, which is why it is so important to discover *your* people when you have a disability. People on the street would laugh at me whenever I struggled to get a cab, and I nearly found myself on the other end of a fist for knocking people over (or their $20 drinks) one too many times. The epitome of this phenomenon happened at a crowded bar, where everyone was pretty much standing on top of one another. I was trying to maneuver my way through the crowd, tilting and craning my head, when I accidentally bumped into someone. Instead of stopping, I kept going—by that point I'd grown accustomed to hit-and-runs. It was easier than stopping to apologize, explain, or face any escalating hostility.

I did, however, stop when someone yelled, "Oh my God, you just knocked over Spidey's girlfriend!" It was Kirsten Dunst, the *Spider-Man* actress. In that moment, I wished I could put on a costume and web-sling away. Somehow, Peter Parker's double life seemed easier to manage than mine.

Dating was also a frustrating part of New York life, as I struggled to find the right time to tell people I was going blind. When out one night with our friend group, plus the addition of the woman I was interested in, Jessica, I asked Ankush to lead me to the dance floor. She was dancing there with Nono.

"Fine, but if you like her, you've gotta tell her about your vision. She'll figure it out sooner or later," Ankush told me.

I rolled my eyes, holding onto a bit of stubbornness, before finally nodding my head. "Okay, fine," I agreed.

"Well then, shoulder up," Ankush called back to me as I put my hand on top of his shoulder and went forward. "Shoulder up" was just one of the many terms my friends and I had collected to direct me around more easily, along with the phrase "get skinny"—which Ankush yelled at me next.

I turned sideways, making myself as small as possible, as Ankush guided me through a tight crowd. The music continued to blast around us, and the flashing lights left me stunned, but after smelling a bit more sweat and feeling the increase of the vibrations on the floor, I knew we had made it to the dance floor.

"Hey," I said to Jessica, whom I found through my peripheral. "I have to talk to you."

She stopped dancing. "Is everything okay? Is this the right place—"

"I'm going blind," I blurted out, panic in every word. Like an awkward idiot, I kept on dancing in the silence that followed. After a minute of no words, I stopped and said, "Jessica?" quietly at first. I couldn't see her anymore in my peripheral. "Jessica?" This time, I raised my voice and spoke with a worried tone, as if I had lost her or something.

Ankush put a hand on my shoulder, which stopped me from calling out her name a third time. "I think she left. I'm sorry, Johnny."

I didn't take it as hard as you might've imagined—the same thing had already happened two times before with two different women. It did, however, confirm what I already believed to be true: No one could know I was going blind.

Secrets Get Revealed

Another thing I appreciated about New York, however, was the subway.

The subway system was relatively well lit, it was routine so that the stops were easy to memorize, and announcements were made over the loud-speaker—often in garbled, semi-intelligible words, but still—there was a predictability to the system. The only thing I had to be careful of was the gap between the platform and train. Admittedly, I stumbled on it a few times.

The fact that I could navigate the subway well while going blind was nothing but encouraging. Because my job for the city took me all over the five boroughs, it was a relief that I didn't have to rely on anyone but myself when I was traveling. To me, the subway represented freedom—which was part of the reason why I wanted to live in New York in the first place.

Travel is often essential to employment, and people with travel-limiting disabilities are less likely to have jobs.[16]

But even that setting didn't turn out to be as glamorous as I had originally imagined.

It was 5 a.m., and I was exhausted. I had to get up early that day because work was taking me far into Brooklyn that morning, and I had a meeting in two hours. I found my way onto the L train subway line and took a seat in an open spot—completely unaware of what I'd find there.

First, there was a feeling of wetness—almost as if I had sunk into a warm pool—and then there was the smell. *I am sitting in urine*, I realized. *I am s-i-t-t-i-n-g in urine.*

Panic followed next. I jolted out of my seat and ran out of the car, my hand covering my mouth to stop my gagging. The subway zoomed away

---

16   Bureau of Transportation Statistics, "Travel Patterns of American Adults with Disabilities," United States Department of Transportation, December 11, 2018, https://www.bts.gov/travel-patterns-with-disabilities.

seconds later, and I was left dizzy by the fast breeze it left behind, full of shame, hating the fact that my slacks were stuck to my skin, and feeling drips down my leg. I rushed out of the underground station and ran back toward my apartment, holding my laptop bag up to my bottom the entire way there.

After I got back into my apartment, took off my pants, and showered about three times, I looked at myself in the mirror. And then I broke into tears.

I was lucky enough to have found a group of friends who accepted me in New York and to have learned some valuable lessons there, like how to navigate the city by using patterns, math, and routines, but neither of those things was enough: I needed to find a place that was actually accessible, or that I could make accessible with enough funds. And in New York, neither was true.

It felt as if New York had just broken me.

So, after months of penny-pinching and slurping recession soup, I was ready to escape the city and find a new job that would take me far away from New York.

Steve Clemens, whom I knew from Bangalore when I worked at Sasken, had called me with an opportunity. He was on the board of an India-based manufacturing company called Aster that was branching into Cameroon and wanted me to help finalize a joint venture between Aster and Spectrum TV, a local television broadcast company. I flew to India to meet with executives associated with the business—they planned to have me guide cell phone tower efforts across Africa—and the interview went great. However, when we went out to dinner afterward, they realized the extent of my vision loss, and suddenly, the company had second thoughts. They ended up backtracking and told me the job was split into two halves (east Africa and west Africa) and that I'd be handling one of them.

They also gave me a six-month deadline to make something out of nothing.

With the weight of all their demands on my chest, I was off to a new place—searching for the same things I had been searching for my whole career: belonging, accessibility, and equity.

CHAPTER FIVE

22,758 MILES

I landed in Yaoundé, the capital of Cameroon, in the middle of the night. I walked in the direction of a man yelling, "Taxi! Taxi!" knowing that he could have been anyone. He could have even been a kidnapper.

"I need to get to the Hilton Hotel," I told him. And after securing my cab, I started to go through my mental checklist: *just the amount I need of local currency in my pocket ... check ... my Nokia phone in my hand, ready to call my parents' number ... also check.* They were thousands of miles away, so there wasn't a lot they could do if something went wrong, but knowing they were on the other side of the line gave me some comfort.

The taxi driver grabbed my yellow suitcase and started pulling it, so I walked behind him, listening carefully to the wheels of the suitcase as the texture of their sound changed. First, they were rolling along the sidewalk, smooth against the concrete. Then, there was a quick gap in the sound before it picked back up at a slightly lower, and more distant, frequency. *Okay,* I noted, *there's a curb there.* I guessed where the curb was based on what I had heard and gingerly stepped off it. Thankfully, I took no spills and was able to find the car based on the sound of the trunk slamming.

My driver zipped me around this new city, where I was able to perceive slices of life: people walking about the city, grabbing food from stands, and cars swirling around me as if they were in a game of Mario Cart—normal city things. Beyond what my vision could tell me, I was able to embellish the picture further based on the sounds and smells around me. The clicking of the turn signal, our car braking and accelerating, the passing loud music from shops we drove by, street hawkers buzzing outside my window, the warm, humid wind whipping in through the open window, carrying with it the scent of fried food and sweets.

The image I was creating was actually nice—full of opportunity and new life—but still, I kept my thumb on the Call button the entire ride.

The car suddenly screeched to a sudden halt, which jarred me. *Where am I? What's happening?*

I was nearing the brink of a panic attack when the driver called back at me, "*Nous sommes arrivés à l'hôtel* Hilton, *monsieur.*"

I didn't understand a word he said, but I did hear the word "Hilton" among it. It was a feeling similar to the relief when I'd drive home safely by following brake lights in North Carolina. I could put my phone away without having to press Call.

"Great!" I yelled exuberantly. After realizing that the sentiment came out wrong, I cleared my throat and tried again, "I mean, good. *Merci—beaucoop? Beaucoup?*"

"*Ouais*, almost," he responded with a chuckle, then met me on the sidewalk with my bags. After paying the driver, I ventured in the direction of the Hilton, rolling my yellow suitcase with one of my hands, as always. My newest adventure was just beginning, and I felt every ounce of the excitement in the tips of my feet.

One of my partners, Colin—the owner of Spectrum TV—was helping me navigate the difficult task of securing my work permit in Cameroon. To do this, Colin had coordinated with a man named Fritz, an employee of his in the city, to take my passport and paperwork to the immigration office. Fritz would need to get several authorized signatures, and because there was no guarantee that everyone who needed to sign off would be in the office, he would have to repeat this process every day until he got it completed. Fritz had warned me not to leave the hotel because the police might harass me (I was noticeable as an Indian guy), and if they found me without a passport, they would take me to jail—or worse.

After completing the work-visa issues, the plan was for me to relocate to Douala, which was the business capital of the country. There, I would start up the new telecommunication infrastructure business between Aster and Spectrum. The need was for galvanized-steel cell phone towers, which were hundreds of feet tall, to be built across Africa, and it was an opportunity for Aster to supply them from their headquarters in Hyderabad, India, where they faced heavy competition in their domestic market. By focusing on Cameroon, it would give them access to a new and budding telecom market and could have big economic potential for them. Of the six countries in the Central African Economic and Monetary Community, Cameroon had the largest economy and could give them a beachhead into the continent. As for Spectrum, it would give them a new revenue stream aside from their broadcasting company, with little risk or up-front investment on their part.

On paper, it looked like a win-win for both organizations.

If my efforts in Cameroon were successful, Aster would look to fan out into other countries.

Of course, things didn't turn out how I expected them to, right from the get-go. I knew if I was going to be successful here, I needed to have a basic understanding of French—even though Cameroon was unique in the fact that it had two national languages, French and English.

I was trying to study up on my French during my fourth night in the Hilton (and failing, of course, because Rosetta Stone uses pictures to teach, which made it incredibly difficult for me to actually use the software), when I got a knock on the door.

It was Fritz, who was returning to the hotel for the passport handover and our nightly drink of pineapple juice. "You're almost done," he said, as he poured himself some juice.

"Oh, thank God," I replied, slumping onto my bed. "I don't know how much longer I can be cooped up in this hotel."

"I said 'almost.' Since you're going to be living in Douala, that's where you need to get your passport stamped."

"Well, that's no big deal. I'll just head over there tomorrow."

"No," Fritz said, shaking his head, "You need to go tonight. Like, right now."

"What? Why?" I felt flustered as I stared at all my clothes scattered around the room. The sudden urge to clean and pack was overwhelming.

"Because it's going to take you all night to get there, and your visitor's visa expires tomorrow. You'll have to take the bus—and you'll want to look nice! You need to look professional so that you can go directly from the bus to the immigration office in Douala."

I quickly threw on my best suit and headed outside with any necessary papers. Fritz managed to help me find the correct bus, and I hopped on, without realizing how long of a trek the ride would really be: 140 miles west. The bus air conditioner was also broken, so all of the windows were open. All I could feel in the darkness was the hot breeze, the thick humidity, and the occasional bug splattering against my face. By the time I actually arrived in Douala, my suit was wet with sweat. All I could think was, *What have I gotten myself into?*

But at the same time, I was always told I was going to have to work twice as hard as my peers because I was a Brown person growing up in the U.S., so I thought this kind of struggle was necessary for my career. And with my diminishing sight, I figured the rest of my path had to be that much more difficult—that I would have to work exponentially harder for the same amount of success the sighted person next to me had. So, as I reflected on my mom's last words to me, "You don't have to do this," before I left for Africa, I thought, *Yes, I do.*

In my mind, I had no other options. How could I find success on those manicured lawns and clean streets of my hometown of Cary, where everyone wanted to live? But just maybe I could find my luck on these crumbling streets that few others would dare to travel, which were laden with obstacles. If only I knew then what I know now: the resources I needed to succeed were out there for me—and I didn't have to go halfway around the world to find them.

Square One

Knowing how long it took me to get a work visa, and the fact that it was going to take me *months* to get a business license for the company, I knew I had to start building relationships with the banks as soon as possible.

We needed funding for two reasons: One, I started the company with a $20,000 investment from the partners, but these cell phone sites would cost several hundred thousand each to build. Also, the potential client, MTN Cameroon—the Cameroon entity of MTN, the largest telecom operator in Africa[17] (think of it as the AT&T or Verizon of Africa)—was looking to build out roughly 80 of them in the first year, so we needed access to millions of dollars to complete the contract. Second, I was working on the request for proposal with MTN, so I had to include in my proposal which local banks I was working with. It didn't matter that Aster had operations all around the globe; it had no track record in Cameroon or in Central or West Africa. I needed the banks to get funding guarantees and a line of credit, so if I won the business with MTN, I could then start to procure materials and goods from vendors located all around the world.

And yet, I struggled to find a banker to support this new venture. I couldn't blame the banks for the countless rejections I received. After all, I was just a guy from the U.S., with no prior experience heading up a company, or even working in Cameroon, and I didn't even have a business license in the country.

---

17   Arne von See, "Mobile Telecom Services in Africa—Statistics and Facts," Statista, February 7, 2022, https://www.statista.com/topics/6700/mobile-telecom-services-in-africa.

If only the banks had seen a study of 140 U.S. companies by Accenture–alongside the American Association of People with Disabilities and Disability:IN—which showed that companies that offered the most inclusive working environment for employees with disabilities achieved an average of 28% higher revenue, 30% greater economic profit margins, and twice the net income of their industry peers, I might not have had as much trouble securing a bank account.[18]

However, after many failed attempts at banks all over the city, where no one would open an account for me, I tried Citibank. I told them how I used to work with Citibank in India when I was with Sasken, so they sent a car to pick me up. The banker I met with was named Amir, and I had nothing to show him but my hopes and dreams. I couldn't even tell him who all my partners were because Colin was a political figure in Cameroon and wanted to be a silent partner. I just had to convince them that I was going to do business in Cameroon.

They ended up being the only bank to take a chance on me.

With a bank account open and all of my papers settled, I was able to get my bearings in Douala. I set myself up at Akwa Palace, a three-star hotel that cost about $200 a night. It was safe, clean, easy to navigate, and centrally located—MTN Cameroon's office was just a quick cab ride away. In fact, the MTN Cameroon executives would often go to Akwa Palace for dinners and events, so I thought if I could stay there and be seen by them often enough, they would believe that I wasn't some type of swindler but, rather, committed to building a company in Douala.

It was exactly what I was looking for—except for the cost. I had an idea and talked to the hotel manager, Elvis.

"I'm building a company, so a lot of people will be coming by here," I told Elvis over a glass of juice. "I'd love to have a relationship, or a partnership,

---

18   "Getting to Equal: The Disability Inclusion Advantage," Accenture, accessed April 28, 2022, https://www.accenture.com/_acnmedia/pdf-89/accenture-disability-inclusion-research-report.pdf.

with the hotel, but $200 a night is too expensive." I tried to look the part in my blazer and suggest the opportunities that could come from hosting me. Even if I couldn't see all that well, I could present an image of keen professionalism—after all, I had watched my father do business my entire life.

Maybe his example rubbed off. Elvis gave me a sweetheart deal, so I ended up paying $40 a day to stay there.

The room I stayed in—and worked out of—was decently sized. It was in the hotel's old wing where long-term residents lived. Across from the bathroom along the length of the wall was a long table meant for a TV, but the table became the office desk. It was a modest beginning, but at least it was the beginning of something new.

Pretty soon, my hotel room became home to my new company. I'd get out of the shower in the morning, get dressed, and then open the door so all my coworkers could file in and start working. We had four people crowded around the makeshift desk, two people sitting on chairs, and one on the bed. The Wi-Fi was spotty, printers were stacked up on the makeshift desk, files filled the refrigerator, and wires were weaving their tendrils around the room like some mutant plant. There was barely enough room for all of us, packed in like sardines.

But even though things felt messy, it was exciting to be at the forefront of something so new. It felt as if I was following in the footsteps of some Silicon Valley entrepreneurs.

One reason the company was able to grow so quickly was—in an unexpected way—due to my vision. People with disabilities are some of the greatest problem-solvers in the world. We are constantly having to figure out creative solutions to problems every single day, no matter whether we are at home, at work, or out in the world. That's a lot of problem-solving practice, which also happens to build up your resiliency.

Creative thinking and resiliency also are qualities of successful entrepreneurs, and a key reason why in 2019 in the U.S., people with disabilities ran their own business to a greater extent than the population without disabilities: 10% of people with disabilities were self-employed compared to 5.9% of the rest of the population. Many highly successful entrepreneurs have disabilities, including Richard Branson and most of the sharks on Shark Tank. [19]

It was those key qualities that happened to be another reason we were able to grow so quickly.

For example, one of the things that was key to my success in Cameroon was my ability to listen to people, so I could then figure out the solution to the problem. When I heard our client MTN had taken the contract that I was bidding on away from a company called Alan Dick, a U.K.–based communications company that had local Cameroonian people on the team, I was quick to snatch them up to join my team. And when one of these early employees suggested I would need a procurement person because getting materials out of the port was difficult, I took him up on the offer, and soon we were a team of eight—and we were doing well.

My success was also due to my naivety of how to run a business. I did it the way that I thought a business should be run, and that concept was realizing that I wasn't the smartest person in the room, surrounding myself with others, and leaning on my ethics.

Finally, I was living my dream: being a CEO. I worked all the time and lived in my office, but it felt great.

One of my employees, Sushanth, became my number two at the company. We were both young—I was 28; he was 26—and we would share our excitement over beers. (In fact, it's one of the few things I learned how to order in French there: *une grande bière pression, s'il vous plait.*) Sushanth

19   Eric Ascher, "RespectAbility Launches Disability Entrepreneurship Toolkit," RespectAbility, August 24, 2021, https://www.respectability.org/2021/08/born-for-business-disability-entrepreneurship-toolkit/.

even became somewhat of a guide for me; I'd shoulder up like with my friends back in the U.S., or he would move out chairs for me to sit. We would play it off like it was a sign of respect—he was going out of his way for the CEO—when it really had to do with my inability to see.

A lot of additional problem-solving arose from doing the job itself. For example, when I tried Microsoft's Windows 7 for the first time, I discovered the operating system had a high-contrast mode, which allowed me to fashion the computer with a black background and white text. In addition to that feature, I had begun using a magnifying mouse, the Microsoft Notebook Mouse 4000. I had 10 of these mice and stashed them *everywhere*.

Between the Windows 7 high-contrast mode and magnifying mouse, I was able to finally feel comfortable seeing a computer screen. It was game changing; technology no longer felt like a hindrance.

I also preferred to go to the same café for meetings and would only go to a specific restaurant where the lighting was best. At both places, I would sit in the same seat and would order the same thing each time. I knew their menus, so everything was choreographed—and when it came to signing documents, I had to trust my team. My secretary would point and put her finger where I needed to sign, so I would feel where she put her finger and scribble my signature. I still sign documents the same way.

More to Life

A few months later, my team and I were officially awarded with the MTN Cameroon contract. It was for over 30 sites out of the total 80 sites, and its value was around $8.4 million. We had a lot to prove to them—and *prove* we did.

With our improving finances and new clients, I was able to upgrade to a two-bedroom apartment in a complex that had two buildings: one for offices and one for apartments. My company started renting the office directly across from me on the fifth floor, and there were now approximately 30 of us.

Even though the company was starting to gain some traction, and we were making money, all I could hear in my head was my dad's guidance, which

I had heard since I was a young kid: "Don't waste company money." Since the company was paying for my apartment and furnishing it, I kept my apartment so bare that there was only a bed in my room and a couch, TV, and stationary bike in my living room. (I was on a health kick, okay?) We even shared an internet cable between the office and my apartment—which meant that there was a long cord hanging between the two buildings, which must have confused people.

One night, when I was riding my stationary bike in front of the TV and watching the *Late Show with David Letterman* on the only channel in English that played shows from the U.S., Jessica Biel showed up on the screen and spoke about climbing Mount Kilimanjaro, the tallest mountain in Africa. The climb was meant to bring attention to the global clean water crisis.[20]

"We wanted to do this thing and really put it out there and inspire people to create their own challenges for themselves," she said. "I actually would hike wearing a weighted vest, a 20-pound vest because I knew I had to carry a 30-pound pack," she continued. "I was hiking all through Vancouver, which is where I was working at the time, and [doing] cardio and eating healthy and everything I could. But what you can't really train for is …"

"That's exactly what I was going to ask you about," Letterman said. "Did you have trouble with the oxygen deficiency? It's not as dense … the oxygen in the air … with that altitude, right?"

"Crazy things happen to you. Your brain can swell. You can feel nauseous. Some people actually on our climb had almost drunk sort of symptoms."

The interview stuck in my head—Mount Kilimanjaro was located in Africa, after all, and it represented something *big*. My life was a challenge. Building my company was a challenge. Living with blindness was a challenge. Climbing a 19,000-foot mountain was a major challenge, but if I could do it, maybe I'd learn to never doubt myself again. Maybe I could also prove that same thing to the rest of the world.

---

20   "Jessica Biel (Letterman)," YouTube video, accessed April 28, 2022, 5:25, https://www.youtube.com/watch?v=7iv3NK7EToo.

I planned the trip with my high school friend Stephen and started training right away—running "suicides" in the long hallway of my apartment or walking up the stairs with a weighted backpack. It became something to strive for.

Blind Insight

The hard work of my team was being recognized and because of our quality and speed of delivery, MTN Cameroon awarded us 20 more sites, for a total of 54. We generated roughly $12 million, and $2.4 million in profit in our first 14 months of operations as a result of that project. Our success caught the attention of MTN, which was the parent organization to MTN Cameroon. During a meeting with some execs from MTN, I explained to them, "You have to stop looking to Europe and South Africa for your solutions and start looking east and west. Latin America and Southeast Asia present untapped opportunities—markets that represent similar geographic challenges as Sub-Saharan Africa."

After that discussion, my budding company skyrocketed forward.

As my company worked with MTN, I showed them how they could make their cell phone towers smaller and cheaper, with less of a footprint and lower costs. I found a simpler way to add even more value to MTN. Through group procurement, my team could cut down our costs significantly, which would benefit all of MTN's subsidiaries across the 20 countries where it operated.

But the gains came with some losses too.

Cell phone tower procurement at MTN was done by another local distributor in Nigeria, and by shifting to our services, that business was out around $9 million. The danger became real when members of that local distributor asked Steve and me to meet them for dinner at a hotel in Lagos, Nigeria's largest city, and they gave us a message: "You're messing with our pockets now."

They didn't need to say too many more words for me to recognize the threat, and I didn't see the need for us to go back to Nigeria afterward.

As our footprint on the continent grew, I found myself flying in and out of Douala several days a week, and it had its own dangers and challenges. Because of my blindness, I had hired a driver named Blais, who was my Murgon in Cameroon. I called him my CTO, chief transport officer. Like Murgon, he never let me out of his sight. However, when it came to navigating the airport, I needed even more support, so I hired a facilitator named Felix, an off-duty cop, to help me through security and handle all my papers.

On a day when Felix couldn't be there to guide me out of the airport, I got held up by some staff just after leaving the plane. They probably recognized me from the many other times I flew in and out, but to be fair, I was also rather noticeable: an American who was often holding onto Felix's shoulders to get around, the same way I navigated the bars and restaurants in New York. I must have been a target for a long time, and because I wasn't with Felix, I was vulnerable.

"*Tsk, tsk, tsk* …," one of them whispered in a thick French accent, "You're not going anywhere yet."

Before things progressed further, I heard my driver Blais calling out "*Arrêtez!*" Suddenly, I felt my attacker's hands leave me and was taken by Blais instead. After calling the group some names in French, he told me, "It was taking you too long to come out, so I came in to check on you. I'm glad I did."

"Yeah, me too." I let out a sigh of relief.

As I walked away to the safety of my private car, I thought about how *lucky* I was—and not just because Blais found me in time. My privilege came in the form of being able to afford a facilitator—and a driver who cared for my well-being when my facilitator wasn't there. What about the blind guy who is navigating the airport alone? Or the woman who is walking by herself with a cane at night? Accommodations sometimes require fortune, which is the most unfortunate thing of all.

I realized another thing that day. I had other dreams I wanted to accomplish back in the States—like going to business school and finding someone to start a family with—as well as climbing Mount Kilimanjaro. Work wasn't worth losing my life over.

I announced my resignation to my company that week and planned to leave my yellow suitcase behind in Cameroon. I wanted to leave my days of traveling the world behind me as I looked toward studying and eventually settling down somewhere in the U.S. I wanted to stop running away.

"Animal" Tamer

As I got ready to leave Cameroon, we began transitioning Sushanth, my second in command, into first command. I thought he was the perfect person to take over the company because of the amount of growth he had exhibited in the past two and a half years: when he was first brought onto the team, he tended to get overwhelmed and yell when things weren't going our way—something I coached him out of.

But that overwhelming feeling had been building up in my stomach more and more, ever since I had announced I was leaving.

After a few weeks of training Sushanth, I took off the metaphorical training wheels and encouraged him to make bigger decisions without me. We were in my office, Sushanth was sitting behind what used to be my mahogany desk and was surrounded by local art that I had picked out and enjoying a cup of coffee together when he informed me of a company update.

"Oh, I forgot to mention this to you—Steve likes the forecast of that new local deal."

"What?" I asked, the coffee suddenly hotter in my hands. "You talked to Steve without me?"

"Wait, should I not have talked to him?" Sushanth replied with urgency, eager to please.

I slowly set my cup of coffee down on the table next to me and got out of my chair—a chair that visitors used to sit in when they were having a meeting with me. A chair that *Sushanth* used to sit in when he was visiting *my* office.

And when the anger completely took over, it felt as if I had lost control of my body entirely. "Remember what your place is here, or I'll put you in your place!" I bellowed.

I stormed out of the room, leaving Sushanth's eyes wide and full of shock. The moment was especially ironic because I had coached Sushanth away from the very behavior I was exhibiting.

I immediately regretted yelling at him. I didn't even disagree with him—I just wanted my control back. It was hard to watch the company I had built be passed onto someone else, no matter how great I thought the other person was. It was also hard to see how well he and the rest of company were doing without me at the helm. Deep down, I had assumed things would fall apart without my guiding the company, but that wasn't the case. They were thriving.

After reconciling with Sushanth and leaving the company behind, I tried to focus on preparing for Mount Kilimanjaro physically and mentally. I still couldn't forgive myself for yelling at Sushanth and wanted to do something about it, so my mom connected me with a friend of hers who was a Christian Science practitioner. She believed I needed to understand my eyes as "fixed" already, perfect as they were, and thought that acceptance would come from *forgiving* but not *forgetting*. And when I could forgive but not forget, it would leave space for me to listen to God. She led me through guided meditation where that concept was the focus.

Breathe in …

Forgiveness that went back to people like Ms. Fenton, my high school English teacher. I had to forgive her. Not forget—*how could I forget?*—but let go of how she and others had hurt me.

I had to focus on understanding and recognize that my blindness didn't define me.

I also had to forgive myself. I carried too much bitterness and frustration inside. I had this irrational sense that I deserved my blindness somehow, or that I'd done something to deserve it. I was angry and resentful about my eyesight, but I was also full of fear—fear of missing out and fear of living an unfulfilled life.

Breathe out ...

I had reached a breakthrough just in time for Mount Kilimanjaro. And even though I was leaving a company behind in Cameroon, I was taking a lot with me: new problem-solving skills, a full passport, and the experience of building a multimillion-dollar company from the ground up.

CHAPTER SIX

24,724 MILES

After becoming hands-off at my company, I headed for Mount Kiliman-jaro. The plan was to summit the mountain first, and then move back into my parents' place in the U.S. for a home base while I spent the rest of the summer traveling all around the world before beginning business school in the fall. After starting a successful company and working so hard for so long, I felt a break was much needed—and I actually had the money to do so. I booked trips to Belgium, Haiti, India, and a few other places to visit friends who were living there. When the season ended and fall came around, it would be time to settle down again and start a new chapter in Washington, DC, where I would be going to grad school.

My friends and I were calling it "The Summer of Johnny." The name had a good ring to it—and it turned out to be true.

After applying with a guide company, my friend Stephen and I flew to Tanzania and got settled inside a hotel that the company had set us up in. The following day, we met up with our tour guides by the poolside so they could check out our equipment. The scent of chlorine was strong enough to sting my nostrils, and the morning sun was bright and hot.

The first guide got up from his squeaky pool chair and said, "Hi, I'm Brighton," with a comfortable handshake.

The other one stood up shortly after and said, "And I'm Bacardi—like the rum."

Stephen and I laughed at the joke. "Nice to meet you guys," Stephen said as he began laying out our equipment on a lounge chair. They had given us a checklist of items to bring that included headlamps, gloves, shoes, hiking sticks, and even the right types of socks.

As I listened to Brighton and Bacardi sort through our equipment, meticulously flipping each item over and checking their functionality at least three times for safety, an unnerving feeling began to grow in the pit of my stomach. Mount Kilimanjaro was becoming very real, very fast—and I was starting to doubt myself, despite the six months of training I had just completed.

"These look good," Brighton commented, pulling away from the equipment.

"Yeah, nice work, you two," Bacardi added. "Here's the plan for tomorrow: We will meet at six a.m. at the base of the mountain, where we will hike for the next eight hours until we reach camp. You guys have chosen the Machame route, which is also known as the Whiskey Route because of its toughness,[21] so you can expect that we will be traveling the same way for the next week."

Yeah, why did we do that again? I questioned, suddenly regretting everything as the lump of nerves in my throat grew and swelled. My vision had only been worsening over time, but Stephen and I had chosen to do the Machame route, the longest and hardest of the hikes, because it was supposed to provide the most impressive views and a variety of habitats. I was praying that I could see enough of the hike—which was supposed to take us through a range of the world's climates, like farmland, rain forest, alpine desert, and arctic summit—for it to be worth it.

---

21   Machame Route website, accessed April 28, 2022, https://machame.com/.

"So, it'll be five and a half days up, and a day and a half down. After each day, we will reach a different base camp, where we will eat and sleep and prepare for the next day's climb. Any questions?" Bacardi asked, after finishing his summary.

My shoulders grew tense as I gave Stephen a look of apprehension; he placed a hand on my shoulder, settling me. "Uh—" I started, my voice as shaky as a little boy's, "You guys should know that I have a visual impairment. I can't see well at night."

It was a little bit more nuanced than "I can't see well at night," but I was too uncomfortable to elaborate. Again, because I wasn't able to clearly articulate my situation, I couldn't properly advocate for myself. As always, I ended up wishing I had.

With a shrug, Brighton replied, "Oh, you'll be fine. Most of the hiking happens during the day anyway."

Approximately 30,000 people attempt to climb Mount Kilimanjaro every year, and on average the reported number of deaths is about 10 fatalities per year. It's very easy to do evacuation via helicopter or a stretcher, which is why there are no dead bodies on Kilimanjaro.[22]

Just like that, my blindness became a minor issue. I wished Brighton had asked more questions—after all, accommodation requires both parties to participate—but I knew I was also at fault.

No matter what impression Brighton and Bacardi got of me the previous day at the pool, the full reality of my situation was very quickly exposed the second we stepped onto the trail. The first day of climbing took us through the rain forest, which meant we would have to traverse a wet, muddy surface.

"Hey, are you okay back there?" Brighton called out from the front of our

---

22   "Mount Kilimanjaro Deaths," Climbing Kilimanjaro, accessed June 30, 2022, https://www.climbing-kilimanjaro.com/mount-kilimanjaro-deaths/.

group, hiking in front of Stephen, as we started up a flight of muddy stairs.

"Yeah … maybe!" Bacardi responded from behind me.

Thanks, Bacardi. That's reassuring, I thought, as I took my first step onto the muddy platform. My shoe landed with a loud *squish* and slid around in the mud for a few seconds before stabilizing. *Okay*, I thought, *that worked. Just go slow*. Unfortunately, my next step wasn't nearly as graceful. My left foot slid forward and sent me into the air, landing on my backside.

"Oof," commented Bacardi, as he helped me up from the ground. "Don't worry; I won't tell anyone you had an accident."

He was referring to my butt, which was now covered in dark-brown mud. I let out a feeble laugh, not really in the mood to joke. "Ha, thanks."

Bacardi learned to hold back his jokes as soon as he realized how serious my vision issues were. I took one step after the other and slipped almost each time. People began to pass us left and right. The humidity started to suffocate me, causing the droplets of hot mist to prickle my skin and pile up on my forehead. It was also impossible to find my footing in the mud, and without anything to grab onto, the ground became my safety net. I even considered crawling up the rest of the stairs. I continued upward at a turtle-like pace, but I rapidly learned that there was nothing I could do to prevent myself from falling. Instead, I just learned to deal with the struggle and my stinging, aching muscles.

The day felt impossibly long, but we did actually make it up to our camp location for the first night. There were five tents scattered around the cleared area, and two of them belonged to our party. (Our porters had gone ahead and set them up.) The wind was rushing down the mountainside like a train, rattling the tents on the land.

I was so exhausted that I could barely talk, and the dried, cracking mud on my skin was so tight that I felt as if I were turning into a statue.

"Good job, Johnny," Stephen told me with an added pat to my back—but even that hurt.

That moment was also when I noticed that Stephen, unlike me, didn't seem phased by the strenuous day.

Bacardi, Brighton, Stephen, and I ate dinner by the fire—some thick soup and bread that the porters had made for us.

Bacardi was the first one to comment on the day. "Good effort today, both of you."

"Thanks for the participation award," I quipped with a smile—hoping to hide the pain I was physically and emotionally enduring.

Brighton looked up from his food and stared directly at me, suddenly very stoic. "Did you know only fifty percent of hikers make it to the summit? Sometimes, Bacardi and I will make bets." He went on, "John, you're a man, and Stephen's *a lion*. You're not going to make it."

I froze in place, dropping my fork. His comment was a jab to the heart—and I couldn't decipher whether or not Brighton was trying to insult me or just prepare me for the inevitable. Either way, Brighton had just become another person who didn't believe in me, which didn't feel good in any realm. He had also just reaffirmed my reasoning behind not telling people about my vision problems—I feared rejection, and it had just happened. Like a lot of people who are going blind, I held onto my vision secret for a lot longer than it was actually safe to do so.

There was, however, another reality that I couldn't see at the time: Brighton had just rejected my eyes—not me—and they were my weakest asset. I was about to learn just how powerful embracing my blindness could really be.

Accenture's Enabling Change report found that 76% of employees and 80% of leaders with a disability are not fully transparent about it.[23]

The next 24 hours were a continuous hell. Our slow pace—due to my

23   Laurie Henneborn and Chad Jerdee, *Enabling Change: Getting to Equal 2020: Disability Inclusion*, Accenture, 2020, https://www.accenture.com/_acnmedia/pdf-142/accenture-enabling-change-getting-equal-2020-disability-inclusion-report.pdf.

dimming vision—forced us to get moving two hours early so we could reach the next base camp on time, which meant we had to take off at 8 a.m. instead of 10. Furthermore, each new part of the hike and change in temperature or climate brought about new issues for me to deal with and solve.

It was already dark on the second night when we arrived at camp. The four of us got our food from our porters and huddled around a warm fire. I ate in silence, unable to talk because of how tired I was.

At the end of our meal, Stephen said, "God, the stars are so beautiful. I've never seen anything like it before."

I couldn't see them, but I envisioned a dark sky speckled with white, the Milky Way streaking through it.

"Stephen used to work for NASA," I added, hyping him up even though I could tell he was already filled with embarrassment. "So, he would know."

With all of us still a bit delirious, the conversation shifted to the cosmos as Stephen talked about space and the universe. "Would you want to go to space?" Bacardi asked Stephen.

"I would love to—I think it's incredible. I can't imagine anything more incredible than looking at Earth from above. What about you guys?"

"Yeah, if I got the chance to, I would," Bacardi responded.

I chimed in too, "Why not?"

"Not me," Brighton said. "If I died there, my soul would be trapped there forever … but the rest of my family and my ancestors would be on Earth. That sounds like hell to me."

I looked up at an empty night sky, the stars invisible to me, and considered what that prison would be like: a prison of isolation, solitude, and loneliness. I started to understand why Brighton was afraid of that fate. It scared me too.

On the third day, everything changed. As we continued our trek upward, the trees got smaller and smaller until there were none anymore. There wasn't enough oxygen. That's when the terrain turned rocky.

I huffed my way up the mountain and had to constantly reach my hands outward for something to grasp onto. Once or twice, my footing got lost, causing me to slip and scrape some parts of my legs. I was back to having bloody shins.

We were nearing the top of the stretch where the hike got even steeper when I reached forward, grabbed onto a rock, and pulled toward it—but this time, the rock came loose. Before I could even blink, my feet had lost their placement and I was heading straight toward a face-full of rocks.

I shut my eyes and allowed my body's instincts to take over, curling myself into a ball. I also felt Bacardi's hands on me, holding me up so I wouldn't tumble down the rest of the mountain.

When I opened my eyes again, I was surrounded by Bacardi, Brighton, and Stephen—whose eyes were wide in shock.

"Are you okay?" Stephen asked, shaking the fear out of me with his hands.

"Yeah, yeah, I'm fine." I looked at Bacardi, whose hands were still on my back. "Thank you."

Brighton had uncertainty in his eyes, as if to say again, *You're not going to make it.*

Bacardi helped me up, and we continued forward as if nothing had happened. I tried to do the same and follow in their footsteps, but the hike was just getting harder, and it was becoming more difficult to see. My throat tightened as I reached for another rock and felt it wobble. I stopped, petrified of that wobble. *I can't go on like this anymore.*

"Wait. Stop!" I yelled. "I can't do this anymore. I mean—not like this anyway. I'm not giving up, but I need help."

"We can do that. Right, guys?" Stephen asked the rest of the group.

"Yeah," replied Bacardi.

"We've got this," Brighton added. "What do you need?"

And it felt so great to be asked that question.

After some brainstorming, the four of us figured out that we could use my headlamp, which had a red-light setting, on the back of Brighton's leg. It would act as a guide for me, kind of like how I used to follow the red tail-lights back in North Carolina.

Everything suddenly clicked into place. I stared at that red light and blocked everything else out. I started to use my hiking poles like a cane. Stephen helped out by running ahead and assessing the terrain so that he could give me an idea of the upcoming path.

"We're gonna do this," he kept saying. Sometimes, he'd even use the special phrases my friends came up with to navigate the bars, like "shoulder up" or "get skinny," that we understood to communicate and maneuver through tight spaces and inhospitable climates back then.

When I would have to go to the bathroom, Stephen would guide me to the holes in the ground that were designated squat pots. He would even line me up so I could take a crap. Now that's love. The group would also tell me, "If you're going to fall, fall to the right," or "Fall to the left," if we were on the side of a cliff.

Later on in the day, we reached a section of the climb that required us to scale the side of a cliff. Where Brighton, Stephen, and Bacardi were slower and scared by the height, I climbed like a monkey because I could feel the rock. I could see with my fingertips.

By the end of the day, we were moving faster than we ever had before, and I even had a new motto: *pole*, or "slow, slow" in Swahili. It just goes to show that using the tools of a blind person will get you ahead faster, on a trail and in life.

Over the next two days, Brighton and Bacardi had a newfound interest in me—they were trying to gather a sense of my abilities and not my disabilities—which was especially nice, knowing Brighton had doubted whether I would've lasted a single day on the mountain. At one point, while Brighton and I were walking side by side up the trail, he asked me, "So, what can you see?"

"I can see through my peripheral pretty well," I responded, "but there's blind spots everywhere else. Kind of like a doughnut."

Brighton closed his eyes, making an effort to visualize what I could see. "How do you usually get around like this?"

"You know, a lot of people think that when you go blind, your other senses become incredible. Like you've become some superhero."

Brighton chuckled at the comment.

"I know," I laughed. "It's kind of ridiculous when you say it out loud. It's not like that at all—not for me anyway. I mean, my other senses have improved but only because I practice with them so much more now. In reality, it's a lot of listening, learning, adjusting, and adjusting again. I usually have to problem solve in a matter of seconds."

I welcomed Brighton and Bacardi's interest with so much openness. I was never one to start or even continue a conversation about my disability, except with my closest friends and family; generally speaking, the less I could say about it, the better. I didn't want to be "the blind guy" or "Johnny, my blind friend"—I wanted to just be "John." But now, I was seeing that my blindness was a part of who I was whether I accepted it or not—and by rejecting it, I was omitting part of myself from the rest of the world.

For the first time ever, it felt good to be seen and understood for *all* of who I was with new people.

At the same time, when I became vulnerable with Brighton and Bacardi, they became vulnerable with me too. These exchanges improved our communication, strengthened our trust, and helped us work better as a team. Best of all, Brighton and Bacardi became better allies because they finally understood what I was going through.

It's a phenomenon I like to call "proximity builds empathy," meaning that by spending time with others and understanding their stories and experiences, you will then have a better understanding of their challenges and value them even more.

We spent so much time talking to each other, bonding, and connecting that I could sense Brighton and Bacardi were gaining confidence in me each day. The four of us became a tight team, and together, we would face the biggest challenge of all: reaching the summit.

More than a Mountain

When you ascend to the summit, you typically leave camp at midnight in hopes of reaching the summit at 6 a.m. so you can see the sunrise. But because my party needed extra time, that meant we would have to leave at 10 p.m. In other words, we would be climbing in the middle of the night when I couldn't see and with even less sleep than usual. I'd struggled with driving in North Carolina, walking through crowded bars, and hailing cabs due to my vision issues at night ... but summiting Mount Kilimanjaro? I was so restless that it was hard to get even a minute of good sleep.

Take a deep breath, I reminded myself. *You can do this.*

At 10, we left camp for the last stretch of trail, just as the fires scattered about were dying around us.

"You ready?" Brighton asked ahead of me.

"Yeah, let there be light," I said with a joking voice, hoping the group couldn't hear the shakiness in my breath.

Brighton turned on the red light on the back of his leg, and then we were off.

I homed in on the light, paying attention to every micromovement it made. With every inch it moved up or down, I followed, basing my movement on the direction it was shifting. I also listened to every command I was given from Stephen and held onto things when I could. But still, the wind was getting stronger, the cold was biting my face, and my breath was getting shorter.

Every step forward was harder than the last, but I kept my head down and continued on. I told myself there were no other options.

I had made it about halfway through our hike (not without a few tumbles, mind you) when I heard Stephen murmur something behind me. "Stephen, what did you say?"

"Urmm …"

"Hold on, let's check on Stephen!" I shouted, causing everyone to stop in their tracks. In the darkness, I found Stephen by listening for his moaning and felt how unstable his stance was.

"I feel sick," he whispered.

Bacardi placed a hand on Stephen's shoulder and said, "That would be the altitude sickness, my friend." Bacardi reached into his backpack and pulled out a number of items—some pills, water, and several snacks. "Stephen, you're going to have to keep on eating and drinking to give you fuel. Energy is the first thing to go with altitude sickness."

I felt Stephen sway back and forth and waited for a response that never came. He was too sick to even open his mouth again. "I'll get him to take these. I've got it." Stephen helped me get this far up the mountain, so there was no way I wasn't going to return the favor.

"Okay, open up," I said.

He replied with a weak, drooping jaw, so I forced the pills and some water down his throat. Afterward, I put some food in his mouth and told him, "You've got this."

I was reassuring him just as he had reassured me days earlier. People began to pass us, which was hard for Stephen to watch, but I didn't care. I was used to people passing me. All that mattered to me was reaching the finish line.

As I tended to Stephen, I began to experience a wave of gratitude. I realized I wasn't the only one that needed help from time to time—everyone did, even a lion like Stephen. For the first time, I saw that I was worthy of not only receiving help but giving it too.

Now that Stephen was able to move again with more water and food in his system, the group and I continued forward—slowly, but forward. The farther we went, the more we'd find the same people who had passed us now stopped on the side of the path, unable to go further. It was like the tortoise and the hare. We kept going, kept pushing, and kept grinding until—

"We're here!" Brighton shouted, his voice echoing around us.

The top. We had reached the summit. *I* had reached the summit.

I couldn't see much, but what I did see was white. I could, however, feel the wind. It was hard to ignore—so clean and cold, the type of air that you breathe in deep until it burns your chest and fills your lungs with excitement.

Maybe I wasn't a lion, but a lion couldn't have done what I did. Innovation comes out of necessity, and I was a man who had leaned into his limitations and adapted to his situation. I had used my past experiences to summit Mount Kilimanjaro. If I could accomplish this feat by accepting my blindness, what else could I do?

We took a picture near a sign at the top of the mountain.

> *Mount Kilimanjaro*
> *Congratulations*
> *You are now at Uhuru Peak, Tanzania*
> *5895M/19341FT AMSL*
> *Africa's highest point*
> *World's highest freestanding mountain*
> *One of the world's largest volcanoes*
> *World heritage and wonder of Africa*

As soon as we snapped the photo, we started moving—we were running late, so we didn't have too much time to soak in the moment. When we reached base camp, we passed out from exhaustion.

It took us two days to hike back down the mountain, and on our last night, we all danced around the fire and gave gifts to each other as a token of our appreciation. Everyone who had gone on this journey was there—the porters, Bacardi, Brighton, and Stephen—and as I hugged each one of them, I thought about how close we had all just become by being vulnerable and open. I also considered how much I had accomplished by leaning on them and accepting their help.

Most importantly, I learned that nothing was impossible on this trip. It felt as if I had conquered the business world in Africa—and now I had just overcome the physical world, the roof of Africa, too.

It was time for me to see what mountain I could conquer next.

CHAPTER SEVEN

32,373 MILES

As I looked out the window from the City View Room on the seventh floor of the Elliott School of International Affairs building on the George Washington University campus, even though I struggled to see the sweeping views of the aptly named City View Room—where the Capitol and Washington Monument jut into view, as well as other monuments that are scattered about—I could feel the magnitude of where I was, the heart of our country's democracy.

Regardless of what I couldn't see, I felt as if I had climbed another mountain to be standing where I was, as an incoming first-year MBA candidate of the class of 2014. Kilimanjaro was still fresh on my mind, only summiting the mountain a few months earlier, but I couldn't stop thinking about the arduous path that I had taken to get to my MBA orientation here in Washington, DC.

I knew from the moment that I took the job in Cameroon that I wanted to return to the U.S. to do my MBA, but after the success we had with MTN Cameroon, I felt as if it was an actual possibility. While working long days in Cameroon, I would wake up at 4 a.m. to find a couple of hours to practice for my GMAT, an entrance exam for advanced business degrees, before others got to the office. With a black screen and white text, I was starting to improve my test scores—and even scoring at the 700 level, which would put me in the top 12%. With my practice tests seeming positive, I set my sights on attending grad school in New York City or Washington, DC, two cities with public transportation that I was familiar with and a great next home after Cameroon. NYU was my top choice. It was also in my old stomping grounds, and there was something comforting about that. I had left the city on such a low note, but I felt as if I could return as a winner.

After several months of studying for the GMAT early in the morning before work, I realized that it just wasn't sustainable, and I needed to really dedicate time to studying and working on my business school applications. With Sushanth showing promise as a strong leader and managing more of the day-to-day operations of the company, I decided to take off a few weeks before my exam and go to my sister's house in Milwaukee where I could study without the distractions of the office. Since I planned on taking the test back home in North Carolina, being back in the U.S. would allow me to adjust to the time change and relax before sitting for my exam.

During this time, I often went to Bruegger's Bagels to study for my GMAT, and the walk there was difficult. It was less than half a mile, but it took me along a busy road, past strip malls and parking lot lanes. When you can't see, you get better at listening to the noises around you—the cars whizzing past, an idling motor, the bicyclist's tires on the cement, the wind rustling the leaves of the trees, the courteous car horn's quick beep, and the obnoxious car horn's blaring beep. I tried my best to avoid setting off those obnoxious, frustrated car horns on my journeys.

After expressing my mobility challenges to my sister, I came back to her house after studying one day and found a new white cane on my bed: an early Christmas gift.

Mildly disgusted, I took a few steps backward—as if my body were repelled by the object. "Susan?" I yelled down the hallway, "What is this? I don't need a cane!"

Seconds later, she appeared in the doorway. "I just thought it would help you on your walks. It's to keep you safe," she explained. Susan was the embodiment of tough love—with my parents traveling so much and the nearly six-year age gap between us, she played a parental role for me. When my mother and father weren't ready to accept my blindness, my sister wanted me to embrace it and own it.

I just wasn't ready yet.

That cane represented something I didn't want to be. I didn't want people to think differently of me, to look down on me, or to pity me. I didn't want to be publicly identify as blind. I was getting accustomed to the people close to me knowing I couldn't see, but I wasn't ready to show it to the outside world. Whereas, when you see someone walking down the street using a cane, the first thing you recognize is not who they are, not their talents, not their personality but the fact that they're blind, just like that guy who used to walk by my neighborhood in Cary.

My feelings at this point were a common conflict for people with low or no vision. I didn't fit my own definition or stereotypes of a person who is blind. To me, I didn't *look* blind—I was young, I dressed nicely, and with some vision left, I usually had an idea where to look when I'm talking to someone—and I wasn't ready to change the perception that people had of me.

I hid the cane under the bed and never took it out again.

Instead of accepting the cane, I focused on my applications. I wanted to come up with a unique application for NYU's infamous Essay #2, which required answering the question "why NYU?" So, I made a replica of my passport. It was a badge of honor for me—I traveled constantly when I was in Africa, to the point where my passport had extra books added to hold all of the stamps. For the essay portion of the application, I included stories that would teach my classmates about my experiences and shared which restaurants or places I'd want to take people. I also included QR codes—symbols you scan with your phone—that would take readers to photos and informational websites. In 2011, introducing QR codes into my composition was pretty ingenious because they were really only starting to become more widely used.

Around this time, I also reached out to George Washington University's (GW) MBA office and asked for more information about their program, stating that I was leading a company in Africa and was looking at different B-schools. To my surprise, they wrote down my contact information, and about a week later, I got a call from Liesl Riddle, the associate dean for the George Washington University School of Business. When I chatted with her over the phone, she told me that she had spent years studying diaspora investment and entrepreneurship, with focuses on Africa and Asia, two places where I had worked.

At the end of our conversation, she requested that I visit the GW campus in a month to meet with her graduate assistants and learn firsthand what their program had to offer. The timing was perfect; I would be able to take my GMAT back home in North Carolina, make the five-hour drive up to DC, and then head back to Cameroon.

When I registered for the GMAT, I applied for the accommodations I had been studying with, including the inverted-color screen and magnifying mouse, but weeks before my exam date, I found out I wouldn't be given everything I requested. Their letter spelled it out for me clearly: they were unable to give me an inverted-color screen, but I could use a magnified mouse and a scribe.

Okay, I thought, *that's going to make things a lot harder, but I can do it.* The fact that my business in Africa was thriving had filled me up with a strong sense of faith in myself, which pushed me to train even harder for the GMAT in the final weeks. I prepped with the magnifying mouse and white screen but found that my score was dropping. The white screen tired my eyes and turned them red, but I continued training anyway—hoping that more time in front of the white screen would build up my tolerance to it.

I showed up ready for exam day: perky after a good night's sleep in my childhood bed, studied up, and with rested eyes. I felt determined to do my best as I pushed my way through those double doors. But my excitement quickly started to crumble.

The proctor led me away from a large room in one part of the building and off to another—a tiny room with one desk, one computer, and no windows.

"This is where I'll be taking the test?" I asked, hiding the disappointment in my voice.

"Yes, Mr. Samuel, and your helper is coming from just around the corner there. Best of luck!"

"Hey, dude," my scribe said as the proctor disappeared. He was a young man with a squeaky voice that made him sound fresh out of puberty.

"Yeah, hi," I murmured as we went into the tiny room and sat down at the desk—I was in front of the computer, and he sat next to me. The nervous pounding in my chest grew as I clicked the screen awake, but it worsened the second I moved the mouse. *You've got to be kidding me*, I thought as I inspected a very normal—nonmagnifying—mouse.

I had eight hours to finish the test, which was twice the amount allotted to the rest of the test takers, but I didn't want to waste any more of it focused on what I was up against. Instead, I strained my eyes for *hours* and *hours* until my head was pounding so bad it felt as if it were going to explode. The sweat was building up on my forehead, the tension was piercing my neck, and my breath was getting shakier as time passed. And the helper? The most "helpful" thing he did was distract me—every time he took a sip of his water, which was frequently, the sound of his swallowing was all I could focus on.

With gritted teeth I thought, *this is never going to work*. Even more discouraging was the fact that people were starting to finish their tests; I could hear their passing footsteps outside the door. Anxiously, I asked, "How much time do we have left?"

"Five hours."

It was three hours in, and people were already leaving. Meanwhile, I wasn't even halfway done. I knew I couldn't work at their speed physically, not with these accommodations anyway. My brain was working fast, but my body just couldn't keep up.

And that made me want to scream until my voice gave out.

With each following question, I felt my confidence dissipate like dust in the wind. The test results I received soon after confirmed my suspicions: I didn't perform the way I had hoped. I would have to wait three months to retake the test.

Even though I didn't have the best GMAT results under my belt, I continued exploring my MBA options as if nothing had changed—after all, I wasn't going to pass up an opportunity to visit Washington, DC. I planned a weekend trip to DC and visited both GW and Georgetown's campuses. When I went to Georgetown's MBA office, I requested more information about their program, and the person at the front desk directed me to their website. On the other hand, I spent a few hours with one of Dean Riddle's research assistants and went out to lunch at a student-favorite spot on the campus. It felt as if they were wining and dining me. GW made me feel like a million bucks, and I decided on only applying to one MBA program after that visit. It is so important to build a sense of belonging for whomever you're serving—students, employees, customers, communities—and make them feel that they are valued.

That's what Dean Riddle showed me that day.

Nearly three-quarters of leaders (70%) feel they create empowering environments where people have a sense of belonging, yet only two-fifths (40%) of employees agree.[24]

Ahead of taking the GMAT a second time, I returned to Cameroon and spent three months training my eyes to use a white screen as I practiced

---

24   "New Accenture Research Finds Leaders and Employees Hold Differing Views on Equality," Accenture, March 5, 2020, https://www.accenture.com/ca-en/company-news-release-getting-to-equal-2020.

and practiced and practiced. Before I knew it, it was time for the test and a trip back to the U.S. This time, I wasn't able to get a test appointment in North Carolina, but the only option was in Richmond, of all places. After flying back home to Cary, my dad drove me up the familiar route on Interstate 95 to my old VCU stomping grounds to take the test—hopefully for the last time.

As I stepped onto VCU's campus for the first time in nearly 10 years, I thought about how this was my chance for the ultimate redo—to get the grade I needed for grad school in the city where I'd failed out as an undergrad. But where I'd struggled at VCU in part because I was hiding my diagnosis, I was going to advocate for myself this time.

"I don't want a helper to read to me," I told the test administrator prior to the test. The reader during the first test was distracting. "But I will accept the magnifying mouse."

"That's fine by me," the proctor responded, "Did you bring the mouse with you?"

"You don't have one for me?" I asked, the panic clear as water in my voice. When the proctor shrugged, my heart sank. I had taken all the necessary steps to succeed this time, but their poor accommodation and communication had gotten in my way.

I turned to my dad, who was a few steps behind me and asked, "Dad, what's the time?"

"Quarter till 10. Why?"

I didn't give much of an answer. "Let's go! We have to hurry."

We ran to three stores before finally finding the right mouse at Best Buy— just in time for my test. With the approved mouse, I got the score I needed, but it was so frustrating. What good are accommodations if they don't actually provide them?

It was an important lesson that stuck with me.

With my GMAT out of the way, I could finally focus on the application process. Even though I originally only had eyes for NYU and had poured so many hours into my passport project, Liesl's outreach to me was that much more influential. I had spent so many years feeling unseen—like how many people with disabilities feel—so when someone like the associate dean of a business school reached out to me and saw me for who I was, it was a huge moment. Similarly, if employers can show this level of excitement to recruit people with disabilities, those candidates with disabilities will be loyal, as I was.

I decided to only apply to George Washington University because of her.

Not only did I apply only there, but I also even sent in my VCU transcript because I felt so comfortable and confident. I thought back to my NC State application, and I didn't want to repeat that. If I was going to go to grad school, I didn't want it to be based on a lie. Ironically enough, I still didn't think disclosing my visual impairment was necessary.

I waited and waited and waited. The silence chipped away at my confidence, and I started to doubt myself again. Maybe this new venture was all a mistake. Maybe I was premature in quitting my job. Maybe Steve would let me rescind my resignation.

But then I got a call from the GW MBA office. Not only were they offering me a seat in the 2014 class, but they also offered me the Mount Vernon Fellowship to go to grad school, which would cover a significant portion of my tuition. I couldn't believe it: I was going to be a fellowship student. *Me*, who barely graduated from high school!

After years of doubting myself, I finally felt wanted.

Over the next several months, I learned more about my MBA class. Out of 114 of us, many of the candidates had experience working or living in Africa—I think my work experience made me fit right in with them. It certainly wasn't my undergraduate grades! You could see Liesl's touch all over the makeup of our class, whose focus was on diaspora in Africa. One-fourth of the class was from India and another fourth was from China. It was meaningful to me that someone like Liesl was considering my talents instead of judging me on the areas where I didn't add up. I had been working and waiting for this new chapter to begin—and now I was here.

Monumental View

As I turned around from looking out on the brightness of the clear blue sky outside the windows of the City View Room, my eyes were slow to adjust to the indoor lighting, but I shifted my focus toward the sounds that were coming from inside of the banquet hall containing the classmates with whom I would be spending the majority of the next two years.

With the start of the first orientation event, comprised of educational presentations that would give us a taste of what was to come, I was so excited … until they started distributing papers and projecting information onto a screen that I couldn't see. It felt like high school all over again.

I scooched my way out of the row of chairs I was in and found a teacher's assistant leaning against the wall. "Excuse me?" I cleared my throat and said, "I can't see the presentation. My vision isn't great."

"Oh, no worries," the teaching assistant responded in a quiet voice, careful to not disrupt the presentation. "I'll take you closer to the front." He showed me to a seat in the front row, and I felt silenced again. Was anybody listening? It seemed as if the same thing happened every time I told anyone about my sight. It was especially frustrating because it already took a large amount of courage to ask for accommodation. Instead of looking for people who might need accommodation or expecting them to speak up, I felt that, at some point, the person on the other end of the line should make an effort too. Through these experiences, I learned that accommodations need to be welcoming; they also need to be offered to everyone and *continuously* asked for because some people won't feel comfortable speaking up the first time.

Later that night, there was a networking event, with prominent and successful figures from previous GW MBA classes attending. I knew I was assigned to sit with a higher-up from the World Bank at my table, so I was excited to learn more about his experience and how I could potentially get a job there too—I was prepared to make the most out of the opportunity.

The only problem was that I couldn't see where I was supposed to sit.

While everyone else enjoyed cocktail hour, chatting and mingling, I was stuck searching for my place card at the tables. Just when I was about to give up on finding my name card, I bumped into someone behind me. A charismatic-seeming woman with blond hair and freckles stumbled backward. "Oh, I'm so sorry!" I said, as she recovered her footing.

"No worries at all," she replied with a cordial hand on my shoulder. "Why aren't you buzzing about like the rest of them?"

"I—I can't see where I'm supposed to sit, actually. I have low vision." I looked away, suddenly wanting to disappear. "Is there any chance you could help me find my seat?"

"Oh!" she vocalized, a bit of surprise in her voice. "Of course. What's your name?"

"John Samuel."

Suddenly, she burst out in laughter and explained, "I'm Dean Riddle!"

My heart sank—just like that, my cover was blown at orientation.

But it turned out to be the best thing that could have happened.

After our surprise introduction, Liesl and I had a candid conversation about my blindness—which I hadn't mentioned in my application or during our conversation. She spent the rest of the evening guiding me around the networking event, and afterward, she connected me with Disability Support Services, which offered a range of accommodations like note-taking assistance.

Over time, I continued to meet with Liesl, and she encouraged me to open up about my vision loss with others, which was something I was still struggling with—I mean, I didn't even want to be near a cane at the time. Nonetheless, I followed her advice and found that as I told others about my disability, some of the stigma started slipping away. It stopped being a taboo topic.

Just like my climb up Mount Kilimanjaro, there was power in being honest and open with my colleagues. People couldn't help me if they didn't know. Asking for help wasn't a sign of weakness—it was a call to help me uncover my talents. I couldn't see well, but I could do a lot of other things. I could climb mountains and go to grad school and live my best life. I just needed help with some things that some people don't have to worry about.

Accommodation Defined

Although Disability Student Services was helpful, it wasn't perfect. The materials I needed often didn't arrive in time, which is a huge issue in classes that only last seven weeks or so. Sometimes, there would be no digital textbook available, and other times, content didn't always show up properly on my tablet.

As a result, I started building up relationships with my classmates. The people on my teams started to realize the value I brought because of my out-of-the-box thinking, so they started to read to me to get my input. It felt nice to know that they weren't just reading to me to be nice—but because my contributions were valued.

Providing accessibility and accommodations for people with disabilities isn't just about doing the right thing. If you think about it, people with disabilities are often problem-solvers and bring different viewpoints to the table—and who doesn't want a problem-solver on your team? Why wouldn't you want input from someone who can help you navigate through the muddy waters of business? Through my grad school experiences, I started to see my disability as less of a weakness and more as an opportunity. Sure, I couldn't see as well as my fellow classmates, but I had lots of talents that could be useful. My classmates helped me recognize that—especially one classmate in particular.

During my second semester, I met Nicole through a mutual friend. She was dating another guy at the time who was located in Chicago, and when I overheard her talking about how she couldn't meet him at Whole Foods because she had a meeting, I offered to join him instead. I met up with him until Nicole could meet us, and they walked me back to my house to-

DON'T ASK THE BLIND GUY FOR DIRECTIONS

gether—they knew I couldn't see. It was the first time I'd really spent with Nicole. A week or two later, she invited me to a party at her house, and after that, we had a series of projects and papers we worked on together.

We had class together, became friends, and started hanging out more and more.

One night, Nicole and I were at a bar together, talking about school and life. It wasn't a date!

When my low vision came up, she asked me, "Can you see my eyes?"

I leaned in close to her, focused and focused on her eyes, and then I saw a vibrant emerald—the most beautiful shade of green I'd ever seen. Her eyes and smile stood out to me. I also could make out the contrast between her lips and her teeth, as well as her brown hair against her fair skin.

She was beautiful on the outside—I could recognize that, even with my failing vision—but there was something special about her. The conversation came so easily, and we found commonalities in our views and ideas.

To try and get Nicole to come over, I used to joke, "Can you teach me how to use my oven?" or "Can you help me match my socks?" One time, after hearing that Nicole liked Easter egg baskets, I ran to CVS and bought a copious amount of candy to surprise her. When I was there, I ran into some guys from school who glanced at the big bags of candy in my arms and asked, "What are you doing with all of those? You know they're going to be half off after Easter, right?"

"It's for a girl," I explained.

"Oh," my friend replied, easily able to understand what I was feeling.

When I got back home, I stuffed some of my socks with Easter eggs. I asked her to come over to help me with my socks, and when she did, she found the candy inside of them.

"Stop it!" she squealed, her laughter echoing around my tiny apartment room.

I would've done anything to make her laugh—I was head over heels for her.

True Kindness, Not Pity

I met Nicole through a friend at an alumni event hosted by the International Business Club, of which she was president. Nicole knew I struggled at networking events—it was hard to figure out where to look when everyone is in a circle—so she stayed by my side the entire night. Even though she was the host, she took the time to introduce me—with pride—to everyone she talked to. She was proud to be with me.

Later on, we made our way onto the dance floor. The music vibrated so loudly that I felt it in my chest. Nicole was dancing in front of me, moving gracefully, and when the lights shimmered around her, she looked like an angel.

Serenity fell on me for a quiet moment, and then it hit me: *I have to tell her how I feel.*

"I think I'm falling for you," I stated with confidence—surer than anything I had ever been in my life.

She laughed it off, saying, "I think you may be drunk. Let's talk about it later."

When she came over the next day, I didn't want to sidestep the conversation. "Are we going to talk now?" I asked.

"Oh," she murmured, realizing that what I had said the night before wasn't just a drunk proclamation of love. She couldn't deny that there was something happening between us, a mutual attraction, but there was a lot to unpack. We talked about my vision loss and how it would continue to worsen. She was currently in a relationship. We also had lots of mutual friends, so if this didn't work, would it be worth it?

The end of our first year required a capstone project with a consulting client abroad, so she went back home to Chicago to drop off her dog for the summer. When she returned, she called me. "Hey, I'm single now," she said.

Wow.

We went out on our first date soon after, where we shared our first kiss on my apartment balcony, which overlooked the Kennedy Center. We didn't want to make a big deal out of it because she was going to be in India for her capstone project pretty soon. Fortunately, I ended up getting an internship offer in India too, and on the weekends, we'd see each other.

My relationship with Nicole was intensifying, and my graduate program was everything I'd wished for. Things were falling into place—until I started looking for a job out of school.

When most of my classmates were getting job offers at the beginning of their second year and had an entire year to enjoy themselves with a job waiting at the end, I was applying and getting rejections late into the interview process. I wanted to get a job at a Fortune 500 company in a leadership development program. I faced round after round of Skype interviews that seemed to go well—I could look at the bright light at the top of my computer monitor and talk—but then I'd go for an in-person interview.

I endured seven or eight interviews before being invited to a large pharmaceutical company's office in New Jersey. It felt like the *Hunger Games* of interviews. It was a two-day event with all of these other prospective employees where the company threw cocktail parties and fun events for us, but a lot of these events happened at night. I advocated for myself by telling them I had a visual impairment and asked for a buddy to serve as my eyes. In response, the company arranged for a woman to attend the parties with me—who was, coincidentally, a former B-school classmate of my old friend Mike from my days in New York. I thought her association with Mike would work out in my favor, but my "buddy" ended up abandoning me every single time. I was at a huge disadvantage at these networking events because I was left all alone. At times, I would be facing a wall unknowingly or struggling to make eye contact with the group I was talking to. That weekend, I also fell down the stairs and dropped my ticket for an event I was supposed to be attending, so I couldn't get in.

The whole thing was a nightmare. No one checked in with me to ask whether I was comfortable or getting what I needed to be successful—instead, I came off wrong and received a rejection letter.

Even though I had learned the importance of embracing my disabilities in Africa, I grappled with what to say about my vision in my following interviews, wondering if the accommodations that companies would provide were going to help or hurt me. The predicament led to a horrible situation where my next interview was held in a little, dimly lit room. Afterward, they took me out to lunch, and when everyone got up to leave, I couldn't see where they went.

When I received my next interview with a consulting firm, I decided to ask for accommodations and advocate for myself. The one-on-one interview went great, but then came a case study interview, where I had to analyze a situation and come up with the most creative solution—something I typically thrived at. I asked if they could give me the case study on my iPad so I could read it. The case study was slated to take 45 minutes, but it took me 30 minutes to read this document.

"It's not even worth doing this interview. We don't have enough time," the interviewer told me.

Other students were getting great offers, and I had nothing. Nicole was one of those people. She was waiting to accept her offer—we thought my job opportunity would likely take us away from DC, which is why we hesitated—but eventually, she had to accept hers too. I had no opportunities after graduation, and I was growing increasingly desperate each day.

Forced into a corner, after I completed my MBA, faculty members at GW's Disability Student Services suggested I register with DC's Services for People with Blindness and Visual Impairments, a unit that helps sight-impaired people like me who are looking for a job or want to advance in their careers.

Applicants could get a free Metro card, so I thought, *Sure, why not?* When I went to register, they required me to take occupational mobility (O&M)

training sessions. And one of the trainings was about learning how to use a cane. *Just do it for the free Metro card*, I told myself with some reluctance.

Even though I was hesitant to use the cane, my instructor was really nice and made me feel comfortable. With a few lessons under my belt, any nerves or embarrassment I had about the cane disappeared. Even I was surprised.

Soon after some training on the cane, I went to meet a friend at a restaurant down the street—without my cane. I'd made the walk a thousand times and knew this route, but this time, I tripped. After stumbling, I cursed a few times under my breath and walked the rest of the way to the restaurant in anger. *How could I have let this happen?* I asked myself. Even though I had only been practicing with a cane for a couple of weeks, I felt that the cane was messing up my natural ability to get around—and now that I didn't have it with me, it was messing with my head and making me weaker! It was becoming a crutch, and I didn't want that.

On the way back from the restaurant, I recognized the spot where I had tripped earlier. I felt the rage build up inside my chest, hot like fire, and when I got home that night, I saw the cane leaning against the wall of my apartment. I felt as if it was staring at me, taunting me.

I took all the anger in my bones—from all the years of feeling less than, hopeless, helpless—picked up the cane, and beat it against my knee. But it wasn't as symbolic of a moment as I would've liked it to be because it didn't snap. The damn thing was made of graphite, so instead, I smacked it around my apartment, hitting it against anything I could find.

When I was completely exhausted from all the fighting, I tried to shove the cane down the garbage cute—and it got stuck. *Just my luck*, I thought.

Expectations and Promises

After some time with no luck job-wise, I reached out to Liesl for help, and she connected me with the founder and CEO of an organization called Homestrings. His name was Alex.

We met at a Starbucks, and the place was dark, cramped, and loud. I worried about bumping into people and spilling their coffee. I was coiling in my own skin, thinking *Where do I put my hand? Where do I put my bag?* I had to use my hand to feel for an empty seat and tried not to sit in the wrong place or bump into someone at the adjacent table.

Alex sat down and asked me what was wrong, because I wasn't looking him in the eyes. *What an encouraging introduction,* I thought, and then explained to him that there was so much light coming in from the window that it was hard for me to see him. The rest of the meeting went well—he was impressed by my background—and we met again at the Café du Parc at the Willard Hotel. We continued meeting in the same seats, and the consistency was helpful—but I wasn't looking for coffee meetups with Alex. I was looking for a job.

Alex said he was going to make an offer to me, so I kept calling. I kept calling and calling, and finally I got the offer to join Homestrings and work in Washington, DC. With my job secure, I felt as if I was finally finding balance in my life. I had my MBA and a meaningful job, and I had met the woman of my dreams.

Nicole and I had big reasons to celebrate—we had figured out where we were both going to live, we both had new jobs, and I was planning to propose.

We went out to dinner that night, and I tried to keep my cool the whole time. The ring was sitting in my pocket, and I kept brushing my hand over it to make sure it didn't fall out of my pocket or mysteriously disappear. On the way back home from dinner, I sent a quick text to our grad school friend and his wife who, unbeknownst to Nicole, were decorating the place with sunflower petals that led to the balcony.

Are you guys done?

Yeah, we're done! they replied.

You've got this, bro!

You've got this, Johnny!

My stomach suddenly dropped. This was real. It was happening.

We entered the elevator, and I listened to Nicole press "9" for the ninth floor. It was the longest elevator ride of my life. It had been a sweltering summer night, and I could feel the sweat cascading down my forehead like a waterfall.

"You okay?" Nicole asked, kind as ever.

"Uh, yeah. I'm fine. Just this heat! Crazy, right?" I cringed and thought, *Why am I having elevator talk with my girlfriend and soon to be—hopefully—fiancé?*

As the sweat continued to pour, I counted the elevator's dings and felt it climb to the sky … two … three … four … five … six … seven … eight …

Nine.

The first things I heard were Nicole's gasp and then her laughter.

"This is amazing!" she yelled.

With a shaky hand, I led her to the balcony where we had shared our first kiss. "Love You Out Loud" by Rascal Flatts was playing, there was champagne on ice, and the view of the Kennedy Center was below us. Before Nicole could put everything together, I was down on one knee, a blubbering mess, with the ring in hand. I told her how much I loved her and her good heart, how much I appreciated all the times she had been there for me—and how much I wanted to be there for her too.

I don't know if the message came across as coherent in person, but still, she said yes.

We went to a bar afterward to celebrate with all our loved ones and danced long into the evening. It was one of the best nights of my life.

But when you're as high up as I was, you have a long, *long* way to fall down.

CHAPTER EIGHT

32,374 MILES

We were 54 feet high, at the top of the Reagan Building, for our wedding. It was one of the most interesting spots in DC. It represented the final piece of the Federal Triangle, a wedge-shaped plot of land that stretches across seven blocks and contains a mix of various government buildings.[25] The Reagan Building—the second-largest federal building after the Pentagon[26]—contained a mix of government and private tenants. The crowning achievement of this massive building was its rotunda, which features a 28-foot domed ceiling.[27]

It was my and Nicole's top pick for our wedding venue; not only was it amazing, but the building was also the International Trade Building, which was fitting for both of us. Sometimes we would even joke that we fell in love over the *Wall Street Journal* in our macroeconomics class.

25   "Ronald Reagan Building and International Trade Center," U.S. General Services Administration, accessed April 28, 2022, https://www.gsa.gov/real-estate/gsa-properties/visiting-public-buildings/ronald-reagan-building-and-international-trade-center.

26   "About the Ronald Reagan Building," U.S. General Services Administration, accessed April 28, 2022, https://www.gsa.gov/real-estate/gsa-properties/visiting-public-buildings/ronald-reagan-building-and-international-trade-center/about-the-ronald-reagan-building.

27   "Rotunda," Ronald Reagan Building and International Trade Center, accessed April 28, 2022, https://rrbitc.com/event-spaces/rotunda/.

Nicole and I stepped out onto the balcony during the reception. As we did, the music quieted behind us and was replaced by the sounds of the city below: cars honking, the buzz of people talking, the whir of cold wind around us. "Wow," she commented, a subtle appreciation of the view that didn't require many more syllables.

It was one of the few moments that Nicole and I had together all night because we were being pulled in so many directions by friends and family whom we hadn't seen in years. It was a moment for us to just appreciate the view and be alone together.

"So, did you have a popsicle yet?" The popsicle stand was our joint idea—an easy way for people to cool down after dancing.

"No, but I need one! No one told me that weddings could be such a work-out."

She laughed and placed a reassuring hand on my shoulder. "Don't worry. We'll make sure you get one when we go back inside."

Earlier in the night, a friend had told me, "Take a mental picture tonight. Step back, watch everyone, and soak it all in because it goes by too fast." So I did: Nicole was standing in her white dress under the bright moonlight, DC's monuments were shining all over the city, and behind us, inside the rotunda, our families and friends from across the world (about 150 of them) were dancing together. In my Indian culture, it's not just about a marriage of two people, but it's a marriage of families.

That was what I saw that night—and it was beautiful.

Trust and Betrayal

My job with Homestrings began with a lot of promise—and a lot of questions.

I was the director of product—I had no idea what that title meant. I understood marketing and tech, but product? Without a clear road map, I decided to experiment by shooting videos, writing newsletters and blogs, and using Twitter to help drive traffic to the platform so that we could learn what people wanted from our platform.

I was the only U.S.–based employee. All five of the rest of the team were based in London. Alex traveled back and forth between continents.

Since I was always an early riser, working U.K. hours was perfect for me. I'd wake up before dawn and work all day until Nicole came home from work. I poured myself into the job. I believed in the company's mission to build a crowdfunding platform that would allow people to invest in projects in Africa or other emerging markets to which they wouldn't typically have access. It was exciting to be in this start-up environment with a focus on diaspora and to contribute to this idea of immigrants investing in their own countries while living elsewhere.

But start-ups also come with financial risks. A valuable lesson I picked up in Africa was to request equity, because I hadn't back then. I didn't get any ownership over the company I helped build, which meant I lost out on a growing paycheck. I kept asking Alex about equity, but he usually brushed the conversation aside and assuaged my fears.

I didn't have a reason *not* to believe in Alex—not initially anyway. He had an MBA from Harvard Business School and previously worked for the World Bank. Alex had an executive presence with off-the-charts charisma, which some might call gravitas. He was introducing me to notable people, lining up speaking events, and getting me invitations to the UN, World Bank, and State Department gatherings. He even included me in board meetings, which were held at the high-end Mayflower Hotel with lots of important people from all over the world.

It felt good to feel so *significant*, but after a few meetings, I started to notice that the speaking points and metrics were always the same. There wasn't a lot of investment volume, and the volume we did have seemed to be coming from Alex's adjacent investment company.

Over time, Alex became harder and harder to track down, even though he wanted approvals to go through him. While most companies were moving toward a more lean and collaborative organizational structure, he wanted to maintain a hub-and-spoke organization, so that everything went through him. I'd submit my monthly invoices, and things would get delayed, but

115

the money would eventually come.

The money finally slowed to a trickle. Around this time the company changed its model too; instead of being a diaspora crowdfunding platform—the mission that made me want to be a part of the organization in the first place—we were now going to be an emerging-market fintech company. Alex brought on some guys who were traditional investment bankers and who spent way too much time watching the HBO show *Silicon Valley*, which was new at the time.

Our team was previously quite diverse, with more women than men, and we all came from different parts of the world, like the diaspora communities we were trying to serve. But when the new people joined, the team became nearly all white men, except for Alex and me. Alex also fired the company's CTO, but the interim CTO was great (and the only woman), so I looked at that as a silver lining.

Throughout the company's ups and downs—mostly downs, to be fair—I held onto hope that things were going to improve in the future. After all, I had a lot to look forward to: Nicole and I had put a down payment on a townhouse in the spring and found out she was pregnant in the summer, after we moved into our new home.

Everything was happening! I was so proud of the family we were building together.

The bigger Nicole's belly grew, the worse things got at Homestrings. Not only was I not getting paid, but the stress of everything was also causing the eyesight I had left to worsen. It always felt as if my vision was disappearing like sand through an hourglass, but now it felt as if someone were tapping on my lid.

I wasn't the only one affected either. The interim CTO stopped working temporarily because she wasn't getting paid, and when she didn't go to work, the money appeared in her account. Like her, I wasn't getting paid, but unlike her, I didn't bring it up right away. I tried to brush away the issue, thinking it was some administrative error and told myself that Alex would pay me next week. I also didn't want to stop working due to my commitment to the company's mission. But more than anything, I didn't want to make waves—if I got fired, where would I go? It was hard enough to find a job after grad school in the first place.

Unfortunately, the pattern repeated the next week and the week after that …

My problems were snowballing; I now had expenses and responsibilities, but I didn't believe in myself and my talents enough to stand tall. As I wasn't getting paid, I kept working harder and harder. *Maybe*, I thought, *if I bring in more money, I can get paid.*

I dedicated all my energy toward sourcing better investments for our platform, like Hello Tractor, the Uber of tractors in Africa, or Flare, which was the Uber of ambulances in Nairobi.[28] Furthermore, I would search the web, looking for articles about start-ups in Africa, and then try to reach out through LinkedIn or by guessing email addresses to the companies that I thought were promising. I was resourceful, and it paid off; I started to build relationships with the CEOs and founders of cool start-ups like Hello Tractor and Flare, which could be great draws for investors to come to our investment platform and, in turn, would then help the business—and hopefully get me paid.

It was wishful thinking. I'm not sure any income would have ever found its way back to me, even if the company were making enough. I just didn't know it at the time.

But work wasn't the only thing happening in my life.

I woke up early in the morning, as I usually did, and reached over for Nicole but found she wasn't there. Her side of the bed was cold, so she must've been up for a while. I thought it was unusual because I was *always* the first person up in the morning.

When I got downstairs, Nicole was sitting on the leather recliner, calmly breathing in and out.

---

28   Hereward Holland, "Kenya's Ambulance 'Uber' at Heart of Siege Rescue," Reuters, February 4, 2019, https://www.reuters.com/article/us-kenya-security-ambulances/kenyas-ambulance-uber-at-heart-of-siege-rescue-idUSKCN1PT0NQ.

"There you are," I said, greeting her with a morning kiss on the cheek. "Are you okay?"

"Yeah," she replied with an exhale. "I'm fine, just hurting a bit."

"Ah, okay." That leather chair was Nicole's favorite spot to lie when she was feeling uncomfortable, so I didn't think that it was unusual in any way. "So, what's on the agenda for you today?"

"A few meetings today, one at 10 this morning and—" she suddenly stopped and sat up, frozen. And then her water broke, all over the leather chair.

"Oh my God!" I screamed.

"It's happening! It's happening!" Nicole joined in. After the initial glee, Nicole became stoic and focused. She fixated on her breathing with a narrow intensity, while I was on the other end of the spectrum—all over the place.

I immediately grabbed a blanket that was on the sofa and started frantically wiping up the floor by Nicole. Then, I moved over to the sink where we had a few dishes from the night before and started scrubbing them with a sponge.

"Johnny, what are you doing?"

"I have to make everything clean," I murmured, concentrating on the plate in my hand.

"What? What are you doing?" she repeated.

"I don't want to leave the house dirty!" I jokingly yelled, suddenly aware of how my panic was affecting me.

Nicole laughed along with me and said, "Let's go. It'll be okay, Johnny," with that smile I always loved.

We stepped outside our townhouse, Nicole's bags in hand, to an unusually warm winter day. The sun was beating down on us—almost as if Heaven was blessing us—when our Uber arrived. A nice old man stepped out of the car and quickly started taking Nicole's bags to the car to put them in the trunk. I joined him at the back of the car, and while I placed my luggage in the car, I whispered, "My wife is having a baby!"

He looked at me first with shock and then with joy. "Wow! I thought you were going to the airport with all these bags! I'll make it extra comfortable for you two."

During that long and exciting drive, our Uber driver carefully navigated around bumps in the road and tried to keep us calm with conversation. When he pulled up to the hospital, he told us that his granddaughter was born there and wished us luck.

Ubers can sometimes be a hit or miss, so I was extra grateful to our driver for going out of the way to make the drive to the hospital special. It was as if everything was lining up perfectly: Nicole felt strong, the weather was magical, and our Uber driver was amazing.

But then there was paperwork.

Nicole started to feel nauseous, so the hospital staff took her to her room right away. I was left behind to check us in, and that's when they passed me the clipboard.

"Oh, my wife actually filled all of this out beforehand online. Did you guys not get that?" I questioned.

"I'm sorry, Mr. Samuel, but the form must not have gone through. We haven't received anything on our end."

With a small sigh, I requested some help and sat down in the nearest chair. There I was, giving Nicole's and my info to a medical student to write down while Nicole was about to give birth to our child in the other room. We went through the paperwork as quickly as possible, but when I was finally done, Nicole was already in stirrups—starting labor without me.

I couldn't help but feel frustrated, but I wasn't going to let the paperwork setback dampen an incredible moment.

Nicole was in labor for only two hours, and then Eli, our little baby boy, was born. I couldn't hold back my tears of joy—and I didn't want to.

Over the coming days, Nicole and I adjusted to our new life with Eli. She would feed him at 4 a.m., and by 4:30 or 5, I would wake up and go downstairs with the baby. I would hold Eli and sit together for an hour or two, me and him against the world. In those still morning moments, I could feel him breathing against me … in and out … in and out … so peaceful, so calm.

We had a balcony window near our kitchen, and sometimes when the light was right, I could see Eli's face. I would stand in that window, trying to catch fleeting glimpses of my son so I could ingrain his image into my memory—I just wanted to see as much of Eli as I could before my eyesight was gone.

As excited as I was to be a parent, it also came with concerns.

Changing diapers required lots and lots of wipes and guesswork, as well as diaper cream. (I'll let you imagine the worst, and the messiest, scenarios that come with changing a baby's dirty diaper or cleaning vomit with low or no vision.)

I tried to rely on routines, like sitting in the same spot or playing with toys that made noise. Bells were always a plus. Button snaps on Eli's clothes were difficult for me, so zippers were easier. There were so many buttons!

We lived in a four-floor townhouse with a lot of stairs. Those stairs worried me. I'd drag my elbow on the railing, remaining cognizant about where I was and how I was holding Eli while trying to maintain my balance. I constantly had to remind myself, *if I can climb Mount Kilimanjaro …*

I made sure to buy a bright orange car seat because the contrast was important. I also made sure we had a stroller I could pull, instead of push—that way, if anything happened and it started to tip, it would hit me in front.

I was buying high-end baby items—only the best, because cost didn't matter to me. But without income, and between mortgage payments and baby items, my account balance kept shrinking. At that point, I realized that if Alex wasn't paying me already, there was no way he was going to start doing so.

I needed to find a new job—and fast.

As I began the application process, I felt that insurmountable doubt come back to me, like an old friend. My stress was piling up, my bank account was getting drained, and my eyesight was fading. Who would want an employee like me? What impact could I have on a company if I was blind?

Unfortunately, it would take me hours to fill out online applications because I couldn't see the questions. The worst forms were on a timer system, so half of the time, when I went to click the Submit button on the application, the system would time out because I took too long. I'd waste an entire day or two filling out a single application.

> In a 2015 survey of job seekers with disabilities, the Partnership on Employment and Accessible Technology found that 82% of respondents had applied online, 46% of whom found the online application process difficult or impossible to complete. Accordingly, 9% gave up and failed to complete the process, while 24% reached out for employer support—and 58% of those who sought support were still unable to finish the application.[29]

It was always the little things. I could climb mountains and start a company in Africa and get my MBA from George Washington University, but I couldn't fill out an online form like everyone else could.

I felt as if I was in a coma. I couldn't do what I wanted my body to do. I was angry, throwing things and crying, whereas Nicole was Superwoman. She was nursing and caring for the baby, while I needed to be rescued constantly. At one point, my mom came up to help take care of the baby so that Nicole could help me with job applications.

After a few months of working without income and being unable to find a job, I approached a board member who'd been asking questions about the company's numbers—a lot of the same questions I had—and told him,

---

29   "New Accenture Research," Accenture.

"I'm not even getting paid." I was hoping he could help me, but he quit the next day.

I approached a few other board members for support, even a former mayor of DC, but they brushed me off, saying that it must have been a misunderstanding, that Alex was too good of a guy. They all wanted to believe in Alex so badly that they turned a blind eye to all the obvious red flags.

With every dismissal I received, I questioned myself further too. How could all these notable names invest in a business that wasn't credible? I thought there had to be something I just wasn't seeing.

I spoke with my mentor Dean Riddle from George Washington University about my issues, and she tried to help however she could. She helped me secure contract work through the U.S. Agency for International Development (USAID), which paid pretty well, but the contract involved graphical and data analysis in Excel, which I couldn't do because I couldn't see the screen. Nicole ended up having to do it after her workdays to make ends meet.

I felt hopeless. I got one job interview, and it happened to be with USAID for a diaspora job within the federal government—something I was strongly qualified for after living in Africa and working at Homestrings.

It was perfect. I had deep experience with investments in diaspora.

To top it off, their office is based out of the Reagan Building, where Nicole and I were married. But instead of waltzing through my interview, as I entered the office door, my confidence sagged. Their offices were a maze of tall cubicles that would be hard for me to maneuver around. To make matters worse, I ran into the door frame as I was walking into the room where I was going to be interviewed. I also had trouble shaking their hands, because I couldn't see the folks with whom I was interviewing.

The more I struggled with my mobility, the less confident I was.

I don't remember the rest of the interview, nor do I know why I didn't get the job—even if I was highly suited for it, there were only a few people working in the diaspora investment space, and there were even fewer who had also worked in the markets we were trying to serve. But I am sure they were concerned how I could do the job if I couldn't even navigate their office.

I worried that my career was over. So, as a last resort, I thought about suing Alex to get my unpaid wages.

My parents' next-door neighbor was a federal court judge, the level right below the Supreme Court. I talked to him because I didn't know what to do. I needed money—I needed something. Maybe a lawsuit would be effective.

"In this case, you may pay a lot for lawyers and not get much back in the end," he told me.

Every avenue I went down seemed to lead me nowhere. Everything cycled back to why: Why did I keep working there? Why didn't I speak up earlier? Why did I let one month go into the next?

Why was this all happening to *me*?

I found myself buried in a deep depression, stuck in a cycle of scarring and helplessness. I didn't believe in myself. I couldn't begin to imagine how to climb out of my misery.

Desperation Multiplied

Alex failed to pay me for 10 months—at that point he owed me $70,000—and I had planned a meeting to confront him at a coffee shop near my house.

Our meeting was set for 9 a.m., but I showed up at 8:30. I wanted to be prepared, meticulously plan out everything I could say, and not let my emotions get the best of me—I didn't want him to see how much pain he had caused me. After getting my coffee, I chose a seat by the window. Typically, I wouldn't sit there because the light was too bright, but I wanted him to be able to find me easily—always sacrificing.

By the time Alex arrived, my coffee was cold, and my words were chosen. I thought I was ready for this face-off.

"John!" he said cheerily, as if he couldn't tell that something was off just by the look on my face. "How are you?"

He always started off with pleasantries—his charisma usually worked in his favor—but I was not going to let myself be swayed. As direct as I had ever been, I asked him, "So, what's really going on with the company?"

Alex paused for a moment, then explained, "I want to pay you, but the company can't right now. I want to make changes … but all the new guys we brought on aren't good. They're trying to ruin the company." He was referring to the guys he had brought on six months ago. I could see clearly through his tactics though: He was trying to play the victim card. How could these new employees "ruin" the company in six months?

I began to see who I was really working with in that moment: a con man. Sure, the business and the money were legit, but he had conned me and everyone around him into believing in him—and that's a con man.

I directed the conversation back to the main issue. "Well, I didn't join because of those people. I joined because of you and our mission. Why haven't you paid me?"

Alex deflected again and refused to take ownership, so I changed my tactic. "I have no money. I have a baby and a new house. Do you know how much I've been through in the past 10 months?"

Alex fell silent and stared out the window. Maybe he was searching for the right words. "How is the baby, by the way?"

My jaw tightened, and the anger swelled within me. That was the first time he had *ever* asked about my son, and he didn't even know his name. "The *baby's* name is Eli," I seethed. "But we aren't going to talk about him right now. Why haven't you paid me?" I asked again, this time as more of a statement than a question.

After rejecting me a final time, he offered, "Why don't we start a new consulting business together?"

A new business? He withheld my pay for 10 months and thought I would fall for that gag? I stared at him with disbelief in my eyes, outraged and shocked.

That was also the moment I realized I was never getting paid—and I broke down into tears.

"Hey, hey," Alex whispered, "You're fine. Get it together." He added a few shushes to calm me down too. "Why didn't you just leave? You should've known."

That pissed me off. He was throwing my loyalty to him and our mission back in my face, as if I shouldn't have been passionate about the work we were doing or trusted him. All of the promises, all of the lies about investments ... *I* should have left? *No, you should've paid me*, I thought.

My desperation to hold onto this job, even with its poor conditions, is a common thread within the disabled community. Many can relate to the struggle of finding a job in the first place, which makes it a lot harder to leave it. That phenomenon leads to the total exploitation of people with disabilities.

> The systemic issue is even protected by the law. As Sara Luterman writes in "Why Businesses Can Still Get Away with Paying Pennies to Employees with Disabilities," she cited the essence of the problem: "[under] 14(c) of the Fair Labor Standards Act, businesses can apply for permits to pay disabled employees well below the federal minimum wage of $7.25 an hour. That amount can dip down to mere pennies in some cases."[30]

But now I didn't even have hope to hold onto. There was no more "waiting it out." After my conversation with Alex, as my tears flowed, I faced the devastating realization that Nicole and I would have to sell our home.

The walk back to the townhouse was only 200 yards, but those 200 yards felt like eternity. It was a gloomy day already, and to make matters worse, it started raining when I stepped out of the coffee shop. The only silver lining

---

30   Sara Luterman, "Why Businesses Can Still Get Away With Paying Pennies to Employees with Disabilities," Vox, March 16, 2020, https://www.vox.com/identities/2020/3/16/21178197/people-with-disabilities-minimum-wage.

was the fact that the rain hid my tears.

I continued down the sidewalk—my feet stepping into puddle after puddle, my body shivering from the cold, my face wet with rain and tears—with a fumble in my step because I couldn't see where I was going. Another reminder that I struggled to even walk like a sighted person. To the left, my favorite stretch of homes appeared, but I couldn't appreciate them. They were 10 beautiful townhomes that looked like ours, all of them a different color in the rainbow, but they only reminded me of what I was about to lose.

It all felt far worse than when I was diagnosed with retinitis pigmentosa. Back then I only had to worry about myself, so I could stay in my state of denial and try to ignore the problem. At this point, denial was no longer an option—it was right in front of my face. I had a wife and a son who depended on me, and I was letting both of them down. I couldn't make money, I couldn't be a stay-at-home dad (I thought), and I couldn't see. What good was I?

When I finally got back home, I stood in my doorway with a puddle beneath me—looking like some creature who had returned from the dead.

Nicole yelled, "Hey! How'd it go?" from the kitchen, but I didn't have the heart to respond. She was getting ready for her second week back at work and to drop Eli off at our $2,500-a-month daycare. When she turned the corner and saw my face, I didn't have to say a word. She knew the reality of our situation had just been solidified.

Throughout my life, there had been moments when I felt down—really down, even—but the grief I was experiencing currently was unlike any other. I was reconciling the loss of my perfect life, our perfect home, and our perfect son growing up in DC. Everything we had known up until this point would have to change, and it was dark, lonely, and scary.

I had officially reached my lowest moment—and I couldn't see a way through the darkness.

CHAPTER NINE

32,648 MILES

Nicole and I had put the baby to sleep at exactly 9 p.m.—being in the brand-new parent routine, we took a lot of pride in our promptness—and were lying in bed together. I was playing on my iPad when a notification popped up from my friend Scot, who had texted, "Hey, have you heard of this guy?"

My interest was piqued. I clicked on the link and saw that it was an article from my hometown, profiling a man named Ed Summers. *Why does this seem familiar?* I wondered, then thought back to a week ago, when my dad had sent me the same article through Facebook. Assuming it was just another of the many, many articles he sent me, I passed over it then. But not this time.

As I parsed the article, I was surprised to learn that a man named Ed Summers worked at a company called SAS, a company located less than a mile from my parent's house, that developed a new software for blind users to interpret data using sound. I was even more shocked to learn that Ed had been diagnosed with retinitis pigmentosa, the same disease I had.

After taking a moment to process my disbelief, I sat up quickly and shook Nicole. "Read this. He lives in Cary."

It felt like fate. I mean, what were the odds that this guy lived in my hometown, had the same eye condition, and worked with accessibility technology? What were the odds that he worked at SAS, one of the largest privately owned organizations in the world at the time, and that they were headquartered in Cary?

I had felt so lost for so long, but now I knew where I needed to go: I had to meet Ed Summers.

I barely slept that night because I was so excited, and the next day, I jumped into action. I tried to track down Ed Summers any way I could: I sent him LinkedIn messages, reached out to people with connections to SAS, and asked friends of my father for help.

When evening rolled around, I had no successful leads.

Still, I waited and waited and hoped that Ed would respond to one of my many messages, but then two months went by—nothing.

Although I hadn't been able to successfully reach Ed Summers, he had still affected the way I was thinking. Learning that Ed Summers had built a successful life while blind in North Carolina meant that maybe I could too. Maybe North Carolina was just as accommodating, diverse, and equitable as I needed it to be.

And so, we put our townhouse on the market one year after we bought it. Even though I thought we were going to grow old and raise a family in our home when we originally bought it, we needed the money.

Right away, we started looking for houses in Cary and found one in my parents' neighborhood. We knew that if we were able to sell our townhouse, we could afford this other location. Excitedly, I picked up the phone to call my dad and told him on speakerphone all about the house, with Nicole by my side.

Before I could even finish my description of the place, I heard a car engine roar and my dad's cell switched to Bluetooth. "Uh, Dad? Where are you going?" I asked.

"To see the house, of course! Johnny, what's the address?"

Nicole and I snickered at my dad's excitement—it was cute! I gave my dad the house's address and explained that it was just two streets away from theirs.

Just as he was about to turn down the street, my dad started calling out a name—loudly. "Morris! Morris!"

"Dad? Who's Morris?" I yelled back. "What are you doing?"

"There was a blind guy walking on the sidewalk behind me," he said. "I thought it was that Morris guy you're trying to get in touch with, but I guess not. He looked at me like I was crazy." I heard the engine pick up again as he drove away.

"Dad," I sighed, "His name is Ed Summers. But please don't go back there—leave the guy alone. He's probably not even Ed Summers!"

Too late. My dad had already completed a screeching U-turn.

That poor stranger, I thought. *He definitely thinks my dad is stalking him.*

Even though my hope was minimal at this point, I still felt my heart flutter just a bit when my dad stopped his car and said, "Excuse me, are you Ed Summers?"

A brief pause. A moment to still be optimistic. I waited.

"Yes, I am."

My jaw dropped.

I heard Nicole's joyful laughter and grabbed her hand—hoping she could ease me through the shock.

"My son's been trying to reach you!"

I listened to my dad's car door shut.

"Could you talk to him?" my dad asked.

"Oh, I guess—all right." The phone was now against Ed's ear, and for the first time ever, I heard his voice. He was talking to *me*. "Hello?"

"Hello! Yeah, hi!" God, I sounded like an awkward middle schooler talking to their crush. *Get it together, Johnny.* "I'm so sorry about all of this—my dad, I mean. Um, I've just been trying to get in touch with you—I have the same eye condition you do. You know, retinitis pigmentosa, uh—" *Dang it,* I thought, *of course he knows what retinitis pigmentosa is, John!* "Well, yeah, anyway—could we meet for coffee if I came to Cary?" *Finally.* I sighed a breath of relief.

There was another pause on his end of the line. Perhaps he was just thinking my offer over, or perhaps he was just taking some time necessary to comprehend everything I had just word vomited.

Ed finally replied in a calm, nonchalant voice. "Yeah, sure. Come on down. I'll give your father my cell number."

One little encounter, and I finally had hope again.

Blind Advice

After struggling for months to connect with Ed Summers, I was finally meeting with him.

We met at a Starbucks located one block away from both of us and across the street from SAS, so it was walkable. Even though it was a Saturday morning, and the weather was nice, I felt unbelievably anxious, as if my entire livelihood and future were riding on this one meeting, because, well, they kind of were.

I got my coffee early and sat outside the shop, hoping that would make it easier for Ed to find me. I sat outside and waited in silence for at least 10 minutes, nervously tapping my feet and wondering how blind dates work, until I heard the jingle of a dog's harness. I jumped to my feet and asked, "Are you Ed?" I didn't see any other people about to take their dogs into the Starbucks, so it had to be him.

"Yes, I am."

I offered a firm handshake, and after a little fumbling to grasp each other's hand, I added, "It's nice to finally meet you, Ed."

What was supposed to be a 30-minute conversation suddenly turned into a three-hour one—and it still felt like only a minute had gone by. We had an immediate connection.

Ed made an effort to get to know me first in order to make me feel comfortable. He was interested in my history in finance because his software pertained to it. Moreover, he shared with me the reason he wanted to work on the software: "to enable people with disabilities to realize their full potential in the classroom."[31] This was something I knew all too well. We also talked about our personal lives—what it was like to be fathers (Ed had two sons) and husbands—and Ed started to give me general life advice too, not just about work.

Toward the end of our long conversation, Ed hopped on his phone to check a few texts. I listened as his iPhone spoke a blur of words to him, lingered, and observed as he casually tapped away and dictated texts. These were things that I couldn't effectively do—I was stuck importing discontinued iPhone cases with keyboards from other countries and trying to treat my iPhone like a Blackberry so I could use it to type.

Before we got up to part ways, Ed took my hands and told me with sincerity and urgency, "If you want to continue your career trajectory, you're going to have to learn—to learn as a blind person."

It was a difficult message but one I needed to hear. I'd spent years trying to overcome or counteract my failing vision with stopgap measures. Instead of trying to acclimate to the sighted world, there was another way.

In the past, my issues with audio listening and other accommodations were always that the software couldn't keep up with the speed of my mind. But after hearing Ed use his screen reader at a 3× playback speed, I wanted to try my hand at it, too, with a program called VoiceOver for iPhone. It allows you to use a multitude of gestures, like tapping and swiping, along

31   Ed Summers, LinkedIn profile, accessed April 28, 2022, https://www.linkedin.com/in/edsummersnc.

with audio cues from Siri to control your phone. Your fingers and ears essentially work as your eyes. It's part of the Accessibility features on the iPhone, so I already had it activated on my phone, but I didn't immediately adopt it because I couldn't use the screen reader fast enough.

A few minutes into using VoiceOver, I realized that I had a long way to go before I would be able to listen to anything near Ed's speed. But this time, instead of giving up on the assistive technology, I decided I would make it work for me.

I began training myself on Audible so I could increase my listening speed. I figured that if I could train my ears with the audiobooks, because I still wasn't fast with the gestures and features of VoiceOver, it would help me keep up with VoiceOver and try the gestures without getting so frustrated if I made mistakes.

First, I started listening at regular speed, 1×, and then I started to pick it up, faster and faster—1.25×, 1.5×, 2×, then 2.5×.

I got up to 3x, which was a little too fast at the time—it resembled the legal information at the end of a TV commercial—so I settled on 2.5×, just fast enough where I could retain the message.

After figuring out VoiceOver, I realized that using my phone was only one thing, but learning how to use my computer was going to be even more critical if I wanted to go back to work. Therefore, I decided to try out screen-reader software for my computer—after all, my eyes weren't going to get better over time. The reader scans every piece of text, every working link, every element on a website (even photos) and describes them vocally in a robotic voice. Problems come in with revolving "carousel" elements that move too fast, or elements like photos that don't include proper meta-data and, thus, don't have any description attached to them.

Unlike with the iPhone, the assistive technology that I needed wasn't natively built into the operating system on my Windows laptop. So, I looked into buying Job Access With Speech (JAWS) because it was the industry-standard screen reader for Windows, but there was a problem: It was really expensive *for me*, because unlike profitable businesses, we were barely scraping by. I battled internally for a bit before deciding that, ultimately, I needed to invest in my future. I picked up the phone and called the JAWS customer service line, ready to place an order.

After some friendly chitchat with the sales representative, he asked me, "Were you at the conference?"

Taken aback, I stuttered. "The conference? Uh, yeah. Yeah, I was there." I had no idea what conference he was talking about.

"Okay, then it's $200," he said.

"I'll buy it," I said, happily providing my financial info to finalize the sale.

JAWS was expensive, and thus a barrier for many people, but there also exists a free screen reader called NVDA, which I didn't know about at the time. The company is trying to bring access to all people because, as you can imagine, not everyone can afford $500 screen readers.

Generally speaking, the cost of accommodations tends to hurt an individual's pockets more than an organization's. The average cost to businesses for accommodations for someone with a disability is only $500, which most companies can afford, so it should never be a barrier to hiring someone.[32]

Baby Steps

Now that I was beginning my screen-reader journey, Ed spent the summer educating and mentoring me. I had a lot to learn.

As Ed had also suggested, I reached out to companies with diversity, equity, and inclusion (DEI) programs, but I didn't hear back from a single company. I felt as if I didn't check off a box that they wanted to fill. Most of the DEI programs were focused on race, gender, or sexual orientation recruitment, and disabilities weren't a priority to them. The folks in these DEI divisions were either in HR or legal departments, so they were looking at DEI as a compliance issue—not a business one.

32   "Benefits and Costs of Accommodation," JAN: Job Accommodation Network.

As nothing continued to move there, Ed was speaking at events about the amount of untapped talent out there and distributing my résumé. Even with his hyping me up, passing out my résumé, and connecting me with these companies, all I got back was crickets—and not the good kind from my childhood summer nights.

One of our family friends was an HR executive who got my résumé from Ed at one of his speaking engagements. Here's somebody who *knew* me, who knew my family, who understood the kind of person I was.

Nothing.

My dad suggested I look at jobs with the federal government, since they often hire people with disabilities, but I quickly realized that the available jobs were limited. The government was hiring people with disabilities for entry-level roles, but I was an executive—not that I currently had the confidence to support that.

I daydreamed of all the things I was going to do in my career, if only I got the chance. After hearing Guy Raz's *How I Built This* podcast interview with Blake Mycoskie, the founder of TOMS Shoes, which is a social enterprise that gives a pair of shoes to somebody in need for each pair sold, I was inspired to make sunglasses following a similar model. Instead of giving away pairs of sunglasses, though, I wanted to have the sunglasses made by people who are blind.

Whatever I was going to wind up doing, I wanted to give opportunities to other people with low and no vision—to lend a hand and to be an ally. Because if I couldn't find a job with my background, what did that mean for other blind people without my education, experience, and privilege? And in a world where we all are so defined by our jobs to the point that people often ask, "What do you do?" before they ask for your name, your career will have a significant impact on your life.

As my sluggish summer neared to an end, Ed offered to introduce me to someone: Jeffrey Hawting, the president of a company called LC Industries. Founded as Lions Club Industries, Inc. in 1936, for nearly 80 years LC Industries had been employing people who are blind.[33] I was excited to meet Jeffery because of his company's reputation, but I wasn't very hopeful. Ed had told me that I should take the opportunity to learn about manufacturing for my sunglasses idea—specifically because that's what LC Industries was known for—so I wasn't necessarily looking to be hired.

I met Jeffery at the same Starbucks that Ed and I always went to. It was hot and sticky that day, a typical North Carolina summer afternoon, so I had thrown on the coolest clothes I had at my parents' house—which happened to be a pair of khaki shorts and a red polo shirt. I typically liked to dress nicely with well-fitting clothes, but my limited options meant I was wearing shorts a few sizes too big and a shirt that I was swimming in.

I expected to talk about manufacturing, but Jeffrey talked a lot about technology services and digital accessibility—which I knew nothing about—and before I knew it, we were having an informal interview. Ed had talked about digital accessibility too, but it still didn't register.

The conversation went fine, but I felt skittish and shaky, and the scraggly clothes didn't help my confidence. To make matters worse, as I was walking back to my parents' home after the meeting, I swiped my hand along my shorts and realized the manufacturer sticker was still attached. *You've got to be kidding me*, I complained to myself, so embarrassed that my cheeks became hot.

I started to feel disheartened again, and since I lacked confidence, the casual walk felt like a rock-climbing expedition where I found myself tripping and balancing and hanging on for dear life.

The second you get even a semblance of an opportunity, you ruin it. Nice work, Johnny.

Partial Acceptance

Nicole and I weren't having any luck selling our townhouse, so we decid-

---

33   "Our History," LC Industries, accessed April 28, 2022, https://www.lcindustries.com/who-we-are/our-history/.

ed in August that we were done waiting to move to North Carolina. The house would sell when it sold. We packed up our home over the next two weeks into a tightly filled U-Haul.

I spent the five-hour road trip doing a lot of thinking, like traversing a ravine, considering every possible path I could take going forward, but each one felt hopeless. It was as if dominoes were falling one by one and crushing the next one in their path, and at the end of the trail, there was just me ... alone.

But there was one thing in my control: my attitude. I remembered what Ed had told me, "You're going to have to learn as somebody who's blind," and I decided right then and there that I was only going to use a screen reader.

Without thinking another second, I told Nicole, "I'm not going to look at my computer screen or phone screen anymore. I'm going to use my screen reader full time." Up until then, I was still relying heavily on my vision to use my computer and phone, even though I struggled mightily, but the words came out of my mouth on their own—there was nothing more to say about it.

And then my phone dinged.

It was an email from Jeffrey, the president of LC Industries, whom I had met at the coffee shop. I listened to it on my screen reader—Jeffery was asking me if I knew anyone who wanted to join LCI as a technology services manager.

Uh, yes! Me!

The stars had aligned for me the moment I fully embraced my blindness. We had an interview set up within the week.

It was my first interview in nearly six months. My first interview since I had walked into a doorframe at the USAID offices. My first interview since I had been cheated out of $70,000, had a newborn, lost a home, and gained a home. The pressure was on, and it was manifesting *everywhere*: I didn't sleep the night before the interview, had an absurd amount of coffee in the morning, dressed in the same suit—which I unfortunately sweat through—I wore when I first met Liesl and made my way out the door.

Upon being dropped off at LC Industries, I immediately recognized the building. It was one of Nortel's old offices, the company my dad worked at for 35 years: the same company that brought my family to Cary nearly 40 years earlier and the company where I had visited as a kid and watched my dad conduct business in a suit and tie.

Thankfully, the fond memories washed over me and put my nerves at ease. I told myself it was going to be different this time.

After pushing through the glass double doors, I was met by the reception-ist's smiling face.

"Why, hello there!" she proclaimed in a deep, southern accent. "I'm Cher-yl, and don't you look handsome. Welcome to LC Industries!"

It was quite the welcome—but Cheryl made me feel at home.

The next person I met was DuWayne, my interviewer and a company exec-utive. I was expecting an old man because I couldn't find anything online about him, but DuWayne quickly surprised me: he was young and charis-matic, someone you wanted to be around.

DuWayne led me through an unexciting hallway until we entered his of-fice. Everything was mahogany, from the big wooden desk to the coffee table and chairs. It reminded me of my dad's old office.

DuWayne and I had a long interview that was mainly focused on my ex-perience in Cameroon—he wanted to understand how I built a company from the ground up there. I got the hint that maybe they wanted me to do the same thing at LC Industries.

After a positive interview, DuWayne shook my hand and said it would take about six weeks for them to make a decision. I was hoping they'd end my anticipation earlier, but everything stayed silent in the coming weeks—de-spite the many follow-up emails I sent.

> *The Bureau of Labor Statistics reported that in 2021, 19.1% of people with a disability were employed, compared to 63.7% of persons without a disability in that same period.*[34]

Exactly 42 days later, they gave me an offer.

Proper Accommodation

The first thing LC Industries asked me was what I needed. That felt good.

I provided my accommodation list, which included my trusty Microsoft magnifying mouse, an iPad, and JAWS.

The orientation featured lots of paperwork, but there was someone there from HR to help me—I didn't even have to ask for their assistance. When it was over, the onboarding manager, Audrea, led me through the building, a maze of endlessly long hallways, until we came upon an office with a name on the door: John Samuel.

This was *my* office.

My office with its floor-to-ceiling windows. My office with a pretty view of the courtyard and a gazebo. I felt the furniture: my mahogany desk like my father's, my leather chair, my circular table with four chairs.

Although it was perfect to me, it wasn't objectively perfect. It was filled with office supplies and a printer—which were great for a sighted person but not for me. These items showed me that even at a company like LC Industries that prides itself on the fact that it is the largest employer of U.S Americans who are blind, there was no one in leadership who was blind. Beyond those helpful but unnecessary items, there was also clutter, papers, and other things that belonged to previous tenants of the room.

"What is all this stuff?" I asked.

"Oh, this office belonged to the past four VPs of sales, so some of it's just left-over," Audrea explained. "Don't worry. We'll get it cleaned out for you ASAP."

---

34   Bureau of Labor Statistics, "Persons with a Disability: Labor Force Characteristics—2021," news release no. USDL-22-0317, February 24, 2021, https://www.bls.gov/news.release/pdf/disabl.pdf.

What happened to the past four VPs of sales? "Uh, why did they leave?"

"They all stayed for under a year. Just wasn't a fit."

That made me feel uneasy. I thought, *Is this office cursed or something?* I swallowed the lump in my throat and responded, "Got it. Thank you."

When Audrea left, I went over to my chair and took a seat. I was hoping for some momentous moment—for fireworks to explode or something—for me to feel as if I had finally made it—but instead the chair creaked and wobbled.

Oh well, I figured, *I'm here.* I spent so long trying to get paid, or get a job, that I wasn't about to complain about a wobbly chair. I would've sat in that thing gladly until it fell apart.

For the time being, I figured out that if I sat at the right angle, the chair would stop wobbling. That was good enough, but when DuWayne came in to check on me, I learned that LC Industries was truly different.

He noticed the chair was wobbly and said, "We've gotta get you a new chair."

It was a stark contrast to Alex.

Organizations that actively employ people with disabilities experience 89% higher retention rates, a 72% increase in employee productivity, and a 29% increase in profitability.[35]

With my chair issue settled, DuWayne offered to take me on a tour of the building. "We can do this a few times in the coming days to help you get your O&M."

O&M ... like orientation and mobility? I wondered. "Yeah, that would be amazing."

After exiting my office door, DuWayne asked another question: "Do you want an elbow?"

---

35   Kasey Panetta, "Gartner Top Strategic Predictions for 2020 and Beyond," Gartner, October 22, 2019, https://www.gartner.com/smarterwithgartner/gartner-top-strategic-predictions-for-2020-and-beyond.

An elbow? What's that? I had heard the phrase before (even though I hadn't been asked it directly) but never understood what it meant. Now that I could feel DuWayne's right arm touching my left arm, it sunk in. "Sure," I replied, then grabbed onto his elbow with my left hand.

DuWayne took me to the manufacturing floor, which was textured to assist with cane navigation, and explained to me that nearly 400 mostly blind employees worked there. I listened to the symphony of noises as flatware was packaged, mattresses were made, and items were shipped off. The machines hummed with electricity and motion. The silverware clinked as they fell into their giant buckets, and a bell chimed every 15 minutes, so the employees knew what time it was.

But my favorite noise of all was the sound of canes as they hit the low walls above them, notifying their users where they were in relation to the machines. Hearing those canes echo against the wall brought tears to my eyes.

I was overwhelmed with joy. For the first time ever, I was receiving help in a way that was normal, not uncomfortable or inaccessible. Furthermore, other blind people worked here, so I wasn't alone. Even though I couldn't see everyone, I could hear people talking and laughing and working with every *ch-ch-ch* and every *ca-THOP*.

Wow, I thought, *this place is designed for people like me.*

But besides DuWayne—who has trouble seeing nearby objects—and myself, no one else on the management side of the company had a visual impairment. All the employees with low or no vision worked in manufacturing, meaning my joining LC Industries represented a shift.

When I started the job, there were certain documents being sent around that were not digitally accessible, although Jeffrey and DuWayne would make everything accommodating. But it was still a learning process for a company that had been serving the blind community for 80-some years.

At the same time, I was also getting more comfortable with my assistive technology.

I had taught myself the basics with my $200 subscription for JAWS, but there was so much I still struggled with, such as using it for Excel, Outlook, and other Microsoft products. I connected with Lee, an IT employee who also happened to be blind, so he could teach me all I needed to know about JAWS.

He spent a couple weeks teaching me JAWS, and during that time, Lee and I got to talking about our lives and shared experiences. "I miss classy watches," I joked with a chuckle. "I'll say that much. I always loved wearing them, but now I don't see the point."

"I feel you on that. I've actually been trying to find a Braille watch."

"Those exist?"

"Yeah, of course they do!" he replied with a chuckle. "Blind people can wear watches too."

Watches always had a special place in my heart, from my Swiss Army watch I bought when I was a 16-year-old bagger at the grocery store, to the TAG Heuer watch my mom bought after the many summers I worked to save up during college, and then finally an Omega Speedmaster that I bought after I had success in Africa. My conversation with Lee reminded me of that. As I looked down at the cold steel watch with the empty black dial on my wrist, it didn't matter if it was the first watch worn on the moon, or if it was flight-qualified by NASA for all manned space missions—it was worthless if I couldn't tell what time it was.[36]

I started scouring the internet for a Braille watch. Then I found the EONE watch. Their watches utilize raised hour markers and two magnetized ball bearings to allow you to feel the time through touch. With a sleek design and range of choices, the EONE watch taught me that accessibility could be sexy too.[37]

One chilly winter morning back in DC, I met up with DuWayne at the airport for my first business trip with LC Industries. "Woah, it's cold out

36 OMEGA Watches: Speedmaster60. Accessed July 28, 2022. https://www.omegawatches.com/planet-omega/60th-anniversary-speedmaster/the-moonwatch-1965.
37 "Accessibility," EONE, accessed April 28, 2022, https://www.eone-time.com/pages/accessibility.

there," I said at the bottom of the staircase. My face was still frozen.

"Yeah, and I still somehow managed to see you chugging along aimlessly through the flurry," he quipped.

"That is impressive, my friend," I replied.

After we shared a laugh, I followed DuWayne up the stairs by holding onto the back of his jacket. I had plenty of experience traveling (and going up the stairs, mind you), but I lost my footing that day and tripped—not once, but three times. I was essentially *falling* up the stairs—not walking up them.

To make matters worse, when I reached the top of the staircase, I ran straight into a wall and bounced off it, as if I were made of rubber. "Oh, man," DuWayne murmured, while I noticed people had stopped to watch. They were probably wondering if I was okay or thought that DuWayne was a jerk for walking me into a wall, but they could've also been thinking I was drunk or that something else was wrong with me.

A couple months later, I went to Wichita, Kansas, with a colleague named Mike—who has a guide dog—to meet another organization serving the blind and tour their facility. It also happened to be one of the coldest days in Wichita that year.

On the way to the facility, we huddled inside the van in our winter coats and watched as the frost spread around each edge of every window. The van screeched to a halt in front of the building, the tires unable to find their grip on the ground, and I assessed the icy terrain outside. Ripples of dark ice, barely visible, and snow covered the black pavement.

You can do this, I told myself with a heavy breath, *you've fared East Coast weather just fine before. This is nothing.*

Except it was *not* just nothing. I had to slide across the parking lot in my Oxfords—arms flailing and legs shaking—when I really needed skates. Mike, on the other hand, was navigating the treacherous ground with ease. Mike and his guide dog made it to the "safe zone" (a.k.a. the walkway of the facility) a good five minutes before me.

"That took you … eight minutes and forty-two seconds," he jested with a laugh. Mike was a blind Paralympian skier, so my slipping and sliding must've been amusing to him.

I leaned over and heaved a few deep breaths. Walking through that parking lot was one of my best workouts in years, so I was proud of myself for making it the whole way without falling. "That has to be an Olympic record somewhere."

"Okay, let's go." Mike patted my back and went inside. I trailed him—or so I thought.

My face was met with a freezing-cold barrier. "Ouch! What? What was that?" I pressed my hands against the material and felt smooth glass, wet with condensation against my hand. "You're joking," I complained out loud, maybe to God. I had just run into the door.

With my head hanging down and my face still half-covered in red, I pushed through the glass door. The first sound I heard was Mike laughing.

"I'm sorry, I just—" he had to pull back his snickering before continuing. "Are you okay?"

"Yeah, yeah. I'm fine."

With a hand on my shoulder, he kindly joked, "I see a cane in someone's future."

Ugh. After I returned home, I met up with Ed and relayed the two incidents to him. I expected him to get a laugh out of the stories, as I had, but he shook his head instead like a disappointed parent.

"We're friends now, so I can tell you this. You've got to get a cane."

"Just for you, Ed, fine. I'll try one out—but don't ever look at me like that again." He made me feel worse than the time my parents caught me sneaking out of our house when I was 16.

That night, I went online and searched for a cane. For a moment, I watched myself from above as I browsed the internet and saw numerous variations of the same thing: a skinny white pole with a strip of red at the bottom and a strap at the top of it. *So, this is who I am now. The blind guy with a cane.*

I still wasn't enthusiastic, but I wasn't going to hide the cane under my bed or shove it down a garbage chute this time. Given the impact that the screen reader had on my productivity in the workplace, I was going to give the cane a fighting chance.

People at the office were surprised when I came to work with a cane a few days later. Although many employees at LC Industries had low or no vision, I hadn't used a cane during my first few months working there. But what kind of business leader was I if I didn't fully embrace this?

Using a cane was awkward at the beginning—not bad awkward, just different. What did people think? How would they react? But as soon as those feelings entered my mind, I thought about how *fast* I was moving with so much confidence and assurance. I thought about the meek, uncomfortable person who would trail their hand along the sides of buildings and railings, who would bump into people on the sidewalk and not know what to say, who would trip and fall over arbitrary obstacles. But with a cane, I was cruising.

I honestly expected to leave my cane in my office, just to keep my promise to Ed that I would try it, but I started using it full time after only a week.

Third time's a charm, I guess.

Before deciding to use my cane full time, I reached out to several of my family members and friends, asking them how they felt about it, because I wasn't sure how comfortable they would be with me using one. My mom was the main person who struggled with it. She clung to her faith that I would be cured and that I didn't need a cane.

Weeks after I began using my cane full time, before we went out to dinner, I asked her if I could use my cane, and she said no. Instead, she put her arm around my waist, held my hand, and guided me through the restaurant. I realized then that her gesture was her way of keeping me safe.

The next time I saw her, though, she didn't say a thing about my cane. Instead, she observed as I navigated throughout the restaurant with a confidence I hadn't felt in years. I was finally free, independent, and she accepted the gain. She got to see her son confident, comfortable, and living as his full, authentic self.

A Blessing Once Refused

Everyone's got their own swagger when it comes to using a cane.

You're instructed to carry the cane in your nondominant hand (in my case that would be my left) and use your dominant hand to open doors. But I usually held the cane in my right hand because it felt more natural.

When I would swipe my cane left to right, right to left, typically the ball of my cane would line up in front of my left foot and provide protection. It became automatic, with the rhythm of my wrist and stride in perfect harmony.

The cane also sent a message to everyone around me. After I attended a conference in San Diego, I met up with my buddy Poonacha, whom I had befriended in India, now living in San Diego. He watched on the walk to a restaurant as drivers saw the white cane and screeched to a halt. I felt like Moses parting the Red Sea.

"Dude, this is magic," he said. I had only been using the cane for a month, and here was someone from my past who had seen me struggle to navigate, now seeing me move with ease and confidence.

The action felt comfortable and easy. It was simple to navigate using the cane and simpler than relying on someone else. It helped seeing others get around with their canes. I wasn't alone—far from it.

There was another big benefit of my new tools: I could finally hail an Uber ride. By the time Uber came into popularity, I couldn't see my iPhone, so I would hail an Uber and struggle to read the instructions or see the car— one drawback compared to traditional taxis, which are yellow. The driver would show up, then get upset when I couldn't find them and drive off in a huff. As a result, my Uber rating was pretty poor.

DON'T ASK THE BLIND GUY FOR DIRECTIONS

With VoiceOver, I could finally receive the commands. And with my cane, they could identify that I was blind and give me the extra care and attention I needed, and pretty soon my Uber rating was back to 4.99.

I was also a bit of a chaotic cane user (and still am). In doorways, I would swing my cane all around so that it would bang against the door frame. It wasn't the most graceful movement, but it did create an office joke: everyone knew when John was coming.

One thing I learned during this time was that you have to make it your own. Even though I didn't complete traditional O&M training, I found a method that works for me. When it comes to a cane, or any accommodation for that matter, it doesn't matter what's right or wrong—the only thing that matters is that your shins are no longer bloody.

With a cane in my hand, I came out of the closet. I was finally and fully embracing myself as a man who is blind.

Funnily enough, that acceptance was when my next adventure came my way. Over time, I found myself being invited to more and more higher-up meetings at LC Industries, but the reason was never explained to me, so I just observed and chimed in when I could. Everything changed when Jeffery invited me into his office after one of these meetings.

"John, are you wondering why you're being invited to these meetings?"

"I mean, yeah, of course I am." I scratched my forehead, still confused even then. "But no one will tell me a thing."

"Well, it's time to give you answers." He sat down in the chair across from me. We were now eye to eye. "We want you to build a new business for us. Your goal is to employ 200 people in three years."

I froze as the shock consumed me. "What?"

He smiled with the pride of a mentor in his voice. "That's right. You're going to build the future of our company."

146

CHAPTER TEN

HOME AGAIN

The task in front of me felt momentous. *If I could start a company in Africa, I can do this,* I reminded myself. *And if I could climb Mount Kilimanjaro …*

But even though I had started a company in Africa, the difference with this new business was the fact that I would be serving a community that I had resisted for so long. It felt as if I owed the community for that neglect, and this opportunity was my way of giving back. In other words, the pressure was on.

In my early discussions with Jeffery and DuWayne, we tossed around ideas like creating call centers, working with a scheduling-app company, or collaborating with an eyeglass manufacturer that crafted a low-vision magnifying tool. All were promising thoughts that would create employment for people who are blind, but I felt as if we needed to dream bigger and not only make jobs but also forge paths for upward mobility.

For the moment, we settled on investigating the call center idea, but I knew it wouldn't be enough.

Stumped and out of ideas, I continued to scribble down my thoughts on an endless list while the weight of this new venture hung on my shoulders, like a looming presence I couldn't get off my back. In some ways, I felt as if I had to change the world with this opportunity, as if it was too good not to.

Thankfully, I had the luxury of time—LC Industries wanted me to make the right move, not the fast move, since the concept was a new space for the company.

LC Industries had brought on an external marketing firm to help with the rebranding of the company from LC Industries to just LCI, along with a new logo. I met up with the two marketing heads over a few cups of coffee in a conference room, one of the many marketing meetings I had requested with them since they first arrived. I had been encouraging them to include more content about the technology services work that we were looking to launch on the site, because when you looked at the current site it was very much about the manufacturing.

"Thanks for meeting me," I said after sitting down. "So, any updates on the things we talked about?"

"Of course, always happy to sit down with you," one of them said. Out of the five people who were there, four of them were very polished and professional women; the only man there was speaking. His name was Al, and he was quite dapper, always wearing a bow tie on his neck as if he had traveled into the future and met us here. "Okay, so we've talked it over with everyone, and we just don't think it's going to work. Yes, LC Industries is becoming LCI, but a name change doesn't encompass your new company. Why make it smaller?"

"Sure, I get that, but I want to leverage the long history and brand recognition of LC Industries. I mean, isn't that what I'm *supposed* to do?"

He went quiet for a moment. "Oh, I see what's happening here. You don't get it, do you?"

"Get what?"

"The organization you're starting is going to bring attention to the LCI brand, not the other way around. You're LCI's future."

I shook my head in disbelief, as if I could shake away the last word he had just said. "*Me?*"

"That's right. The move from LCI Industries to LCI is also supposed to encompass the direction the company is heading in. Tech services is that direction, which is basically you and your company."

"Sorry, I just—I'm just a little surprised. I thought this was just going to be a side project. Like a side 'brand,' I guess?"

"No," Al explained, "you're going to be the face of this whole thing."

The stakes had just shot up exponentially. If I failed now, it wouldn't just be my failure. I would be failing the people I was trying to employ, my trajectory in corporate America, and LCI.

Thankfully, that pressure didn't make me want to implode. It made me want to excel.

I jumped into action after that meeting. I reached out to two of the biggest companies that originated in North Carolina, Duke Energy and Lowe's Home Improvement, and pitched the call center idea, which would be done by people who were blind. Duke Energy was interested. They had me come visit along with some blind call center agents who worked in LCI's customer service department, but when we tried to use their systems, I realized that they just weren't accessible.

It showed me that companies could have the best of intentions and want to hire people who were blind or have a disability, but if the systems and processes weren't accessible, we wouldn't be setting any one up for success—not the employee or the employer.

That's when the epiphany hit me: If we wanted to create jobs in tech and have true upward mobility, we had to address the accessibility issues first.

Maybe *that* could be the solution we would provide.

Removing Obstacles

Now with a firm direction and the beginnings of a mission, I needed a team. The space allocated for my new team was located in the old customer service area that was newly renovated. It had high ceilings and long windows, and it was full of 50 empty cubicles, but it was going to have to change. The vacant seats were intimidating to me at first, standing as some kind of reminder of the long road ahead of me, but I quickly grew to see the area as an opportunity, like an open field that hadn't been tilled yet.

The first person I needed to hire was a digital accessibility analyst. One of my colleagues was interviewing a woman named Vahn for an open position in customer service, and during her interview she'd mentioned that she knew HTML, the programming language for websites.

"You should really talk to this person. She may be a good fit for your team," my colleague said.

Vahn was tiny, standing 4' 10"—her cane was so big, and she was so small. She had never formally worked before. She lost her sight because of cataract surgery when she was young. Vahn graduated from college and had lots of knowledge, and for five years, she did accessibility and usability testing for different big-name companies, but they were using her services for free. It reminded me of my treatment from Homestrings, how Alex had taken advantage of me because he knew I didn't have as many opportunities outside the organization.

Vahn became my first employee.

In building out the team further, I recognized we needed some more help. Carla was working in the LCI Customer Service department right before I brought her over. She and I had actually joined LCI the same day, so we had a connection. She was visually impaired her whole life and was color-blind. She actually was from western North Carolina but had grown up going to the boarding school for the blind in Raleigh (Governor Morehead School for the Blind).

I thought she would be a good fit, so she was the first employee I hired after Vahn.

That was my initial team. We were a motley crew.

With a team in place, we figured out a method for accessibility testing and got to work searching for our first client. Developing our process for accessibility took us nearly nine months—it was a long process with lots of trial and error. We got great support from an organization called Lighthouse Works in Orlando, which did some digital accessibility work and gave us some training. We took that training and refined it so that we could then scale it to the levels we needed.

When we were finally ready to launch, I figured our best bet would be a local company, so I went on Google and searched "Raleigh + accessibility." Simple enough. Among the search results was an article about Raleigh Little Theatre, which had been making sensory-friendly shows accessible for people with cognitive disabilities.

I clicked around on their website and noticed that even though their shows were accessible, their website was not.

And then I saw the name of the theater's executive director: Charles Phaneuf, a high school classmate of mine. We were friendly in high school but hadn't talked in nearly 20 years. I reached out to Charles and explained what we were trying to do, and I asked him if we could do an accessibility audit of the theater's website.

He said yes.

Through partnerships like the one with the theater, we were finally able to settle on digital accessibility as a main focus for the company. It was a huge breakthrough moment for us that gave us a sense of purpose and direction. We aimed to focus on clients with a similar mission, who were realizing after one conversation with us that their accessibility efforts weren't making nearly as much of an impact as they could have because of their websites.

After that, we hired Shannon, who has such great energy, a contagious laugh, and a yellow lab guide dog named Tracker. Then we hired Tristan as a digital accessibility analyst. He was very technically sound and incredibly smart but hadn't gone to college and was completely blind. Last, we brought on a recent graduate named Alyssa. It was her first job.

After Alyssa came on, I looked out with pride at the five now-filled seats outside my office. This was our team. It was a solid, strong team—a group of people who deserved better.

We called ourselves LCI Tech.

Recognizing Stagnation

Business began to slowly trickle in, but we didn't start out with a home run. Instead, we were building up a reputation just a bit slower than I would've liked. The contracts were small, so the progress was slow.

In the midst of our incremental growth, Jeffery introduced me to the diversity, equity, and inclusion (DEI) director at the Raleigh Chamber, which was planning their inaugural DEI Conference. The DEI director had compiled a task force that was made up of nearly 20 companies in the area, but none of them had identified with a disability—all were in HR or legal roles at their companies, whereas I was on the business side. Jeffery had asked the president of the Chamber if there was representation from people with disabilities on the task force, and that simple question was when they realized that they hadn't thought about disability in the planning—hence my eventual invitation. It was during one of these task force meetings when I was asked to speak and share my experiences as a person with a disability.

During my panel participation at the conference, I made the argument that accessibility should be more widely considered as part of DEI and supported it with research, financial projections, and my experiences. That little platform was the start of something beautiful. I started getting more and more opportunities to speak and even built-up a following.

I now had a platform to speak to the DEI professionals. Ironically, Ed had suggested a year earlier for me to reach out to them, but they didn't get back to me because I didn't fit their idea of "diversity."

It was the start of my getting invited to speak and build a name for myself in the Research Triangle Park.

I knew we couldn't afford to stagnate, though, so I ventured to a tech conference in Durham next in hopes of better understanding tech companies in the area and meeting people who were interested in collaborating on accessibility. I found myself sitting alone after my colleague went to a networking event. (I didn't feel comfortable networking—I was still getting used to navigating in unfamiliar places with a cane.) So I wound up listening to Donald Thompson, the CEO of a company called Walk West. He was giving a presentation about DEI in a business context and how it could be profitable.

God, he talks like I do, I thought. But he wasn't talking about disabilities.

He offered to meet anyone for coffee afterward, but I didn't feel comfortable stumbling through a room full of haphazardly organized chairs to introduce myself to a stranger. I knew someone who also knew Donald, so I messaged Sharon Delaney McCloud, whom I had met earlier after my Raleigh Chamber event and was a partner at Donald's firm, to make an introduction—a much easier process than my months spent trying to track down Ed Summers.

As we sat down and talked, Donald made an admission, one he'd work to rectify: "I never thought of people with disabilities as part of DEI, and I never thought of people with disabilities in tech." It was a common oversight—people typically think of diversity and inclusion in terms of race, gender, and sexual orientation, but disability inclusion needs to be part of that conversation.

Donald took our conversation to heart, and he started popping by the office and having people on his team connect with us. My hope was that he wanted my team to ensure that the websites Walk West was building were accessible, but there were bigger things at play.

I didn't know it at the time, but a partnership was brewing. Donald was a serial entrepreneur and was working on launching a new business called The Diversity Movement. He later introduced me to a team member of his named Mike Iannelli, who took a deep interest in my team too.

During our meeting, I talked to Mike about my EONE timepiece. I let him touch the raised hour markers—a triangle at 12, elongated lines at three, six, and nine, and two magnetized ball bearings that travel on recessed tracks. I told him about the ball on the inside that reflects the minutes and the ball on the outside that tracks the hour.

"What's great about this watch is that anyone would want to wear it," I explained. "It's sleek and sharp *and accessible*. I want people to see that accessibility can be sexy."

"I see what you mean," he said. "I'd wear that watch."

Just 18 months after that meeting, Jeffery, Mike, Donald, and I decided to launch a joint venture between LCI and Walk West.

But what to call it? We went through a couple iterations. Mike came up with the name Enabler, in the sense that we hoped to enable the disability community as well as companies, but the word has some negative connotations. I considered Leveler, like we were leveling the playing field, but there was another company out there with a similar name.

By October 2020, through LCI's partnership with Walk West, we had a new brand for our joint venture: Ablr.

Ablr was game changing. With Mike and me working together, we started bringing in bigger projects.

But what would Ablr's mission be?

I kept coming back to the mission of Aravind, the largest eye-care provider in the world, and how simple it was: "Eliminate needless blindness."[38] I

---

38   Aravind Eye Care System. "Our Story." Aravind Eye Care System, March 31, 2022. https://aravind.org/our-story/#:~:text=Aravind%2C%20with%20its%20mission%20to,organisation%20remains%20financially%20self%2Dsustainable.

wanted a mission statement like that, something straightforward, simple, meaningful, and profound.

We settled on a mission I'm really proud of: Removing barriers for people with disabilities. We are attempting to fulfill that mission through three major criteria that are based on my own lived experiences:

#1 Eliminating the Digital Divide

I'll never forget how hopeless I felt whenever I was applying for a job. No matter whether it was after grad school or after Homestrings, that feeling was a severe barrier to entry that threatened the well-being of myself and my family. Our digital accessibility services aim to make digital content accessible so that all people can access it. We focus our efforts on adherence to the Web Content Accessibility Guidelines (WCAGs), as well as usability. Having people with disabilities on our team is a key differentiator, because we can provide authentic insight into a user's experience. But our efforts are about more than just websites.

#2 Changing the Mindsets of People in Organizations

One of our larger goals—one that remains ongoing—is to coach companies as they change their culture so that it's more inclusive for people with disabilities. Whether that means asking people if they need accommodations or presenting different tools or resources, it feels as if I'm addressing all of the experiences and challenges I've faced throughout my career.

For this objective, we developed an online course that will train companies on disability inclusion. Because of it, we are hoping that there will never be another person who is abandoned by their buddy at a networking event or isn't able to complete a case study in time for an interview because of improper accommodations.

Our course, called Putting Untapped Talent to Work, goes through the history of disability, disability etiquette, the business case for inclusion, accommodations, and assistive technology. We also provide disability inclusion advising services throughout the employee journey—from recruitment, hiring, onboarding, retention, and promotion.

I've mentioned "proximity builds empathy" before, but it is also influential here: The more we can share people's experiences and stories, the more we can change mindsets. Proximity builds empathy, which is a topic I also focus a lot of my speaking on, is about spending more time with people different from you so that you can better empathize with their challenges.

#3 Creating Pathways for Employment

With the two goals above (eliminating the digital divide and changing mindsets), we are building up demand. This goal is about building up the supply of talent to meet that demand.

This pillar is dedicated to adults—experienced workers and students alike—but is specifically geared toward young adults with disabilities who might be coming out of college, or who might have failed out, or didn't even think about higher education, and are searching for a place where they belong. I want to make sure that no one else has to run all around the world to find that place.

Additionally, we're working on a program that will help companies with internal mobility, as well as connect recent grads who are disabled with allied companies and prepare them for the world they're stepping into.

Our first line of workforce development is focused on creating digital accessibility analysts, because we know firsthand the need for more analysts and because such jobs pay well. The second line is training people to get jobs in customer service and to use Salesforce, which is pretty accessible out of the box and used by so many companies.

Through Ablr, I have effectively taken the struggles I've endured throughout my career and used them to help others avoid similar problems. I want to make the world more open and accessible. I want to make life easier for others who are like me, because I know how difficult it can be.

More than ever before, I was empowered by Ablr's mission. It was even more empowering to think that my boys (plural, Nicole gave birth to our youngest son, Ethan, in 2018) will be stepping into a world that's different from the one that had held me back for so long.

We Are Not Alone

Remember my favorite slogan, "Accessibility can be sexy," that first came about because of my watch? Well, I learned down the road that my watch was created by an MBA student at MIT who noticed his classmate was blind and couldn't tell the time. Yet again, *proximity builds empathy!*

These two ideas were the impetus behind #DripMyCane, one of Ablr's most fun initiatives that aims to get people talking about disabilities while making the topic approachable enough to build empathy. Those at EONE—even me—do a video about their watch. EONE loved the idea of #DripMyCane, and they are now a partner.

Even though I became more and more comfortable using a cane, it still felt like a barrier sometimes, especially at networking events. The world is still getting used to seeing an executive who is blind and uses a cane, so people worry about saying the wrong thing.

On the other hand, when people see a guide dog, there's a feeling of "oh, how cute!" and are naturally drawn to the dog. They want to pet or talk to the dog even though the dog is technically working. A cane, on the other hand, often brings up a different emotion—it's utilitarian. It serves an important purpose but isn't inherently captivating.

We wanted to change that impression, and that's how we came up with the #DripMyCane contest. Ablr and Walk West teamed with a digital marketing company, Creative Allies, to host a cane design contest for White Cane Day, which is celebrated every October 15.[39] [40]

In our first contest, we received about 100 different cane designs from all over the world in all sorts of colors and elements and ideas. The winner featured colorful graphics of sunglasses along the length of the cane. It's the kind of design that could get people talking—and that was the whole point, to get people talking.

---

39   "Drip My Cane," Creative Allies, accessed April 28, 2022, https://contests.creativeallies.com/dripmycane/.
40   John Samuel, "Win $500 Cash Prize #DripMyCane Design Contest," LinkedIn, September 24, 2020, https://www.linkedin.com/pulse/win-500-cash-prize-dripmycane-design-contest-john-samuel/.

Ablr is working on several important initiatives beyond #DripMyCane, including one that pairs four high school students together—two with vision impairments, two without—for the purpose of solving real-life business problems. The project, which is called the Ablr Works Teamship Program, is a partnership with an amazing organization called District C, and we are preparing students for the work of tomorrow.

The program has multiple benefits. The students who are blind get experience working on a team as well as substance to add to their résumés, while the students who don't have disabilities are going to build empathy by working with students who they previously might not have been exposed to—something that will stick with all of them wherever their careers take them. Furthermore, the companies that take on these students as interns will gain a new perspective and hopefully reduce stigma toward employees with disabilities.

That's how we're breaking down barriers.

Clear Focus

My mentor Ed Summers has a goal of touching a million lives, and part of me feels as if I'm a force multiplier of him.

And that's the real aim of Ablr—to touch other people's lives.

It's been four years since I started using a screen reader, four years since Jeffrey Hawting gave me an opportunity, and four years of achieving successes I never could have imagined. The successes are a reflection of my mentors, all of the people who gave me a chance and believed in me when I didn't believe in myself.

I'm thankful for these achievements and that I love what I do, but I still pray every day to God, asking him, *please don't let it all vanish before my eyes.* I grapple with taking vacations and taking days off because I remember what it felt like not to work.

I know what that hopelessness feels like. That fear is an unfortunate blessing because it drives me to do more—because I don't want anyone else to feel that way.

Ablr is my silver lining. Seeing the blue lettering and reddish-orange accented Ablr sign—which was specifically designed with color contrast in mind for those with low vision—immediately outside of my building as I walk into the office brings a proud grin to my face. Coincidentally, the curved line that bridges underneath the *A* and the *B* of "Ablr" matches the daily smile on my face. It is a place where people are actually happy, can grow and learn, and aren't burdened by boundaries. At Ablr, everyone has a seat at the table—sighted or blind, abled or disabled.

During meetings, I listen to the voices of our incredible team as they talk, collaborate, and dream together. Our most recent hire is a South African man who lost his sight in combat while in Afghanistan. Then there's Shannon, who is growing into a young leader, and Kim, a sighted woman who had been working in the accessibility field for over 20 years and acts as my right hand. There's also Sarah in her first role ever, who has jumped headfirst into accessibility advocacy and immersed herself in that aspect; an intern named Courtney who has never had exposure to people with disabilities before; Susanne, who identifies with having invisible disabilities and had been out of the workforce for many years; and Morgan, who has dyslexia and is helping build our workforce development. Last, we have my partner Mike, who used to be focused on surface-level corporate missions but has now found a mission that has changed his life.

Even when I look out at our team—Vahn, Tristan, and Alyssa aren't with our team anymore—they represent what we are trying to do. They have gotten great jobs with McDonald's, CVS, and Pearson's accessibility teams—jobs they might not have ever had if they didn't get trained with us. Even Carla, who is now the front-door receptionist at LCI, is still contributing to our team. Angus became an employee after he had called LCI looking for a call center job, and Carla is the one who convinced him to look at Ablr instead.

All these people are the beating heart of Ablr.

And then there's me at the head of the table, watching them build a better world with their ideas, watching as their words form skyscrapers on the table, and watching as they think of what is yet to come.

But you don't have to work at Ablr to be a changemaker: You can be one right where you are, right now. If you're someone who isn't directly connected to the disability community, you can find ways to be an ally, be part of a better future, and advocate where you can, whether that be at your organization in DEI, out in the world, or both.

If you are part of the disability community and are struggling to find your spot, I want you to find hope and solace in the fact that there is a path out there for you and there is a way for you to achieve your dream. And when you do, remember this: bring people up with you in an elevator, not alone on an escalator.

Your Mount Kilimanjaro is out there somewhere, waiting for you to climb it—and it might just be in your backyard.

ACKNOWLEDGMENTS

To my dearest Nicole, I can't thank you enough for your love and encouragement in sharing my story—your fingerprints are all over this book, and it would still be a draft if it weren't for you! To my little guys, Ethan, and Eli, thank you for your love of reading, and inspiring me to write this book.

I am incredibly thankful for my parents. Mom, for instilling a faith in me that allowed me to take risk. Dad, for being a person of action and willing to stop random blind people on the road; I've been learning from you my entire life how to be a leader, and I couldn't have asked for a better coach.

I'm blessed to have so many wonderful people in my life. Mr. & Ms. G, thank you for being another set of parents to me, and showing me that there was a world out there for me to explore. Mom Lynn, thanks for being my biggest cheerleader throughout the book writing process and holding me accountable. Susan Cohen, thank you for always pushing me to be my best self, even when I resisted. Sarah Varughese, thank you for being another big sister and helping to make my transition to New York that much easier. Thank you to the Chandy Family, who paved the way for my dad to come to the United States, and the next generation who has helped me navigate my own new world.

Ray Mathew, thank you for being my oldest friend, and keeping me out of even more trouble, because this story could have gone a completely different direction.

To Jon Frazier, Siddharth Sura, Scot Humphrey, Stephen Jeffress, Freddie Sexton, Tim Hammond, Juan Carlos Rodriguez, Oktay Rifki, Anoopum Gupta, Vishal Arya, and Emily Fite for being my old friends, and sticking by me through the low times and the high ones.

Thank you to Andrea Hernandez-Tobar, Arben Zeqiri, and Maria Paula Jaramillo for giving me an excuse to visit Uganda, and a sense of friendship that I needed.

Thank you to Brighton and Bacardi and all the porters who helped me summit Mt. Kilimanjaro and giving me a story that I will never forget. A special thanks to Stephen Jeffress for believing in me and my abilities, even when I didn't.

For giving me my first taste of professional success, thank you to everyone on the Aster, Spectrum, and MTN teams. Special thanks to Sushanth Talasila for being the best Number 2 I could have ever asked for, and Edwin Mantsha for opening the door for us to prove ourselves. Most importantly, thank you to Steve Clemons for taking a chance on an unproven kid, and entrusting me with the role of a lifetime.

Thank you to those on the Sasken team who looked past my name and welcomed me with open arms, including Ninan John, Narayan Mandayam, Shrinivas Kulkarni, Priyaranjan, Venkatesh Srinivasan, Indumati, and Akash Jalan. Special thanks to Sri Kannankote and Poonacha Machaiah for taking me under your wings, and John Estrada for seeing that I had a story before I even knew it.

Thank you to Mike and Merina Landau, Yasmin Safdié, Natasha Khanna, Noemie Prot, and Alice Boulez's for giving me the quintessential New York sitcom friend group, and a special thanks to Ankush Khanna for giving me a couch to sleep on, even after ghosting you in college, and Javier Tourne for being the best thing I ever got off of Craigslist.

Thank you to the George Washington School of Business, which made me feel like I belonged from the very first email to my first step on campus. An incredibly special thanks to Dr. Lisel Riddle for being the most influential educator ever in my life, and Dr. Annamaria Lusardi for teaching me not to regret drinking more champagne. And of course, there are my classmates who helped me overcome the social and academic accessibility barriers that was business school, including Amanda Cassiday, Nathan Morris, Juhi Chadha, Shireen Alhasawi, Christen Thomas, Kevin McCarthy, Melinda Moyo, Vina Verman, Frances Spencer, Alissa Medley, Ranjani Sridharan, Yewande Fadarey, Samarth Morzaria, Exeter Jones, Martin Nossett, Eric Miller, Greg Brace, Rohan Shetty, Shivan Agrawal, and Goran Vojvodic.

Business school would not have been complete without my relationships with Danny Arevalo, Kari Huske, Samuel Lewis, and Maria Christina. Couple-friends were only something I had seen from the outside, until I met you all, and I loved every bit of being part of it.

Thank you to Ed Summers for introducing me to the world of accessibility and showing me that my dreams weren't dead—not to mention, my story would not be as compelling without meeting you.

I will never be able to thank Jeffery Hawting and DuWayne Gilbertson enough for picking me up out of the gutter and setting me up for success in my career after I thought it was over. Your kindness and generosity are something that I will never forget.

Thank you to everyone who worked on the LCI Tech and Ablr team. This has been the greatest ride of my career, and it has to do with every one of you, including Vanh Vue, Carla Smith, Tristan Bussiere, Alyssa Cheese-man, Quan Leysath, Kevin Erickson, Ronak Patel, and Morgan Cates. A tremendous thanks goes to the current Ablr team, which I'm so blessed to work with, side by side. Shannon Garner: One of the best decisions I ever made was bringing you back to the team, because watching you grow into a leader has made everything worth it. Kim Casey: One man's trash is another person's treasure—you weren't necessarily trash, but you are our team's treasure. Susanne Meyer: Thank you for bringing my vision for a disability-inclusion course to life, which I know will make a true impact. Angus Kola: It makes me happy to see you find a home at Ablr, where I know you can reach your immense potential. Sarah Clark: It's been amazing to see how you have embraced accessibility, and I know that this is just the beginning of an amazing career. Mike Iannelli: You were the missing piece to the puzzle, and I am so thankful to call you my Cofounder and friend.

None of our successes at Ablr would be possible without the support of LCI, including Bill Hudson, Patrick Lindsey, and Marisa Chrismon, but most importantly the people who work on the manufacturing floor, distribution centers, and retail locations, because without them, there would be no investment in our business.

Special thanks to Walk West and The Diversity Movement for helping to amplify my message, including Annie Snarski who just might be the only person who I know that tunes in to my LinkedIn Live show, and Jackie Ferguson for helping to bring the Disability Inclusion: Putting Untapped Talent to Work course to life. An incredibly special thank you to Donald Thompson for meeting me for coffee and leaving breadcrumbs for me to follow in my quest to building my own personal brand.

Special thank you to Sharon Delaney McCloud for believing that I had a TED Talk worth spreading and a story that needed to be shared.

Thank you to Lindsay Wrege, Michael Evans, and the entire 321 Coffee team for welcoming me in as a part-time coffee bagger.

Thanks to EONE, and the Bradley timepiece, for showing me that accessibility can be sexy. A special thanks to Daniel Ly for his commitment to creating a sustainable product that the disability community can be proud of.

From the moment that I heard about Aravind Eye Care, I knew I wanted to be associated with this amazing organization. Thank you to Donna Campbell for making this a reality.

A sincere thanks to Kyle Johnson and Ramsey Spencer at Lighthouse Works, and to my accessibility mentor Lori Samuels, because without you all, I wouldn't have known the first thing about starting a digital accessibility business. And to Charles Phaneuf and Kathleen Louis for giving us a chance to prove ourselves, because we wouldn't have a business if we didn't have our first clients.

Thank you to everyone on the Book Launchers team who helped make this book a reality. Special thanks to Julie Broad for caring about providing an accessible customer experience and making my choice to work with Book Launchers an easy one, and Dan Good and Kate Hefner for being the best guides I could have ever asked for and helping me bring my story to life.

Last but not least, thank you to all the shoulders, elbows, and hands that have guided me through my journey, as well as all the drivers, including Murgon, Blaise, and the countless Uber, Lyft, and taxi drivers—I will never be able to tell you how thankful I am, but I will pay it forward with my actions.

START SEEING ACCEPTANCE AS A POWERFUL RESOURCE FOR CHANGE

Start embracing accessibility as part of your Diversity, Equity & Inclusion strategy: **johngsamuel.com**

For special discounts or bulk purchases to share this book with others, visit: **baronpublishing.com**

Invite your organization to join me on the journey: **johngsamuel.com/speaking**

CONNECT WITH OUR COMMUNITY

 /johngsamuel

 @johngsamuel

 / johngsamuel

 @JohnGSamuel

THANK YOU FOR READING!

If ***Don't Ask the Blind Guy for Directions*** was helpful, please leave a review on Goodreads or on the retailer site where you purchased this book and help me reach more readers like you!

Printed in Great Britain
by Amazon

10667212R00098